I0459461

INDIE AUTHOR CONFIDENTIAL 3

SECRETS NO ONE WILL TELL YOU ABOUT WRITING

M.L. RONN

ABOUT THIS SERIES

This isn't your typical writing self-help book. This series is a compilation of lessons learned from an indie author trying to walk the path to success. Follow author M.L. Ronn (Michael La Ronn) as he navigates what it means to master the craft of writing, marketing, and running a profitable publishing business. Learn from his successes and failures, and learn about things that most successful authors only talk about behind the scenes.

To read all the collected volumes of this series in an anthology, visit www.authorlevelup.com/confidential.

CONTENTS

BECOME A TECHNOLOGY-DRIVEN WRITER

BECOME A DATA-DRIVEN WRITER

BECOME THE WRITER OF THE FUTURE

IDEAS YOU CAN STEAL

INTRODUCTION

This volume covers the fourth quarter of 2020—the year to end all years.

I don't know about you, but I'll be glad to see the end of this year. It was my best year ever for sales, but it was emotionally difficult. I'm looking forward to seeing what 2021 brings.

Volume 2 of this series covered my efforts to improve my author infrastructure so that I could have a more stable business heading into 2021, as well as the start of my "Beast Mode" challenge, where my goal was to write as many books as humanly possible.

This volume is decidedly more marketing focused. I harvested a lot of opportunities that I planted for myself in Volumes 1 and 2. I wanted to finish 2020 strong.

In fact, my "challenge" for the fourth quarter was "Amnesia Mode." What if I woke up one morning, knew nothing about marketing, and had to learn it all over again? I tried to challenge the marketing knowledge I already knew to see if I could push myself to another level.

. . .

My Core Strategic Priorities

As a refresher, my mission is to create content that entertains and/or educates my audience, preferably both, while staying nimble.

I do this by focusing on five strategic priorities:

1. Become a world-class content creator
2. Become a world-class marketer
3. Become a technology-driven writer
4. Become a data-driven writer
5. Become the writer of the future

I believe these five priorities are the most important for me to have a long-term sustainable career.

What's in This Volume

In the previous volume, I discussed my "Beast Mode" Challenge. In this volume, I'll share what worked, and a very real and unfortunate price I paid for writing so many books in a short amount of time.

I share my journeys into "Amnesia Mode" and some important marketing actions that helped me make a lot more money this quarter.

I also stumbled upon the rare opportunity to give a TED Talk, and I had to prepare a pitch. To use the cliché, I pitched like my life depended on it. I'll find out the results by the time I publish the next volume.

Last time, I described natural language processing and how

I believe I can use it to create a tool to help me catch errors that my editor has made in the past BEFORE I send them to her. I made some more progress in that area.

I also took a new job in the corporate world, one that forces me to use Microsoft Excel at a master level every day. That has done wonders for my data analysis adventures.

I also detail my 2021 strategy and how I plan to start the year strong. I share all of my tactics in nitty-gritty detail. Hopefully, you'll find something useful in it.

And, as always, I came up with some pretty unique and interesting ideas for you to steal too.

There's plenty to explore, and hopefully, this book will inspire you to think differently about your writing business.

Thanks for reading this very experimental series. My sincerest hope is that it helps you in some way.

M.L. Ronn
Des Moines, Iowa
December 5, 2020

BECOME A WORLD-CLASS CONTENT CREATOR

SETTING AS AN ECOSYSTEM

I'll start off this volume with a craft lesson.

I am a big fan of British-Canadian thriller author Arthur Hailey. Hailey is lesser known today, but he was a household name in the 60s and 70s, with one of his books, *Airport,* made into a 1970 major motion picture with Burt Lancaster and Dean Martin, among other stars.

Hailey's books focus on events taking place in a single location. *Airport* takes place in an airport, featuring employees of the airline industry. *Hotel* is a thriller with events taking place almost entirely inside a historic hotel in New Orleans, Louisiana, with the hotel's assistant manager as the hero. *The Moneychangers* takes place in a bank, with bank employees as the heroes. I love the branding and consistency. Hailey is an amazing storyteller too, using the five senses and other mega bestseller techniques to keep you hooked. To this day, I'm amazed at how an author could make *airports* interesting!

Something I learned from Hailey is the concept of setting as an ecosystem. He is masterful at switching between POVs of various workers in the setting. *Hotel,* for example, follows the assistant manager, the bellhop manager, several guests in the hotel, and other employees who work behind the scenes in the hotel. You really get a sense of the place, and that all of the characters are playing their part in the ecosystem.

Most settings are not this prominent, but it would be a fun opportunity to write a story similar to Hailey's where the setting is so front and center. This could especially be fun in a science fiction and fantasy setting.

BOOKS AS PRESENTATIONS OR COURSES

I released eight nonfiction books this year.

I did a talk around my book *Mental Models for Writers*, and it went well and led to decent book sales afterward.

I also did another talk around my book *Be a Writing Machine*, where I took the main ideas from the book and turned them into a talk.

Then I had the idea to structure my future talks around my books. I can easily turn most of my writing books into a talk if I wanted to.

I may start declining speech requests unless I can tie it to a book for a couple of reasons:

- It's easier for me to prepare the talk because I already know the material.
- The talk is better received.
- I have a clear call to action at the end, which is to buy one of my books, which attendees usually do.

It's just an idea at this point, but the more I think about it, the more I like it. It could mean fewer speaking engagements, though.

VIRTUAL EVENTS

I don't often receive speaking invitations, but because of the pandemic, I received more speaking invitations than ever.

I suppose it's because I don't have much of an international reputation yet, so I'm easier to book. I couldn't do many in-person events because of my full-time job anyway.

But I did three speaking events this year. I enjoyed them. Two of them asked me to submit a pre-recorded presentation, which I collaborated on with my video editor. One was a live talk.

I love public speaking, mostly because I enjoy hearing from people and listening to their questions. I always come away with more from Q&A than the talk itself.

I do wonder if virtual events are here to stay. It's hard to imagine many venues going back to big in-person events—not the way they used to. The speaking industry has changed irrevocably as a result of COVID-19. I believe in-person conferences will be smaller, *and* online. I also believe that in-person events won't have the same intimacy and closeness that they used to. There will be a day when people look back on speakers speaking to arenas of thousands of people and remark how those were the good old days.

Anyway, I spent a lot of time preparing for the talks I did this year, and I welcomed the opportunity.

Dedicating a video editor to the talks was above and beyond, and a little unusual—most speakers would never do something like this. They'd just turn on their webcams and speak. Quite frankly, my videos probably stuck out in an odd way compared to other speakers at the virtual venues. But I see this as a resume builder, so if I do a good job with my virtual talks, I can send 10-minute segments to potential venues in the future and give them a *really good* representation of what I would be like in-person. I can also build a "portfolio" of talks. Hell, I could even record generic talks and *license* them to virtual events, and then create bonuses specifically tailored for the venue's audience...wow, I better stop before I give too many secrets away...

That's the way I believe things are going. I could have one pricing structure for venues that want to book me for prerecorded virtual events, another structure for talks that require me to present live, and another for in-person events. Each requires a certain amount of time, money, and resources.

BEAST MODE LESSONS

In Volume 2 of this series, I discussed my Beast Mode Challenge and I promised to share how it went.

On August 1st, 2020, I set a goal to write as many books as humanly possible until October 31, 2020. The main reason was because I hadn't published much during the early days of the pandemic, and because my sales had increased, I wanted to sustain the increase.

I wrote seven books:

- Indie Author Confidential, Volumes 1-2: Secrets No One Tells You About Being a Writer
- 250+ Writing Tips, Vol. 1: A Comprehensive Guide to Writing, Publishing, and Marketing Your Book
- The Reader's Bill of Rights: A Manifesto on How to Treat Readers Right
- The Indie Author Atlas: Your Guide to the Five Continents of the Writing World
- The Indie Author Bestiary: An Epic Guide to Slaying the Beasts of the Writing World

- The Author Income Problem: Track Your Sales Without Pulling Your Hair Out

You can find all of the books at www.authorlevelup.com/books
More results:

- I wrote around 220,000 words.
- I blogged my daily word counts, and my audience loved it so much that I continued blogging after the challenge.
- I did a livestream "writing sprint" on YouTube that was so successful, I continued doing it on a monthly basis.
- In August, I managed to keep writing, even when a powerful derecho storm knocked out power to the entire state of Iowa for a week. In fact, I wrote over 100,000 words in August *alone*.
- I kept momentum on a family trip to my hometown that lasted three days, writing while on the road.
- I had to prepare for and teach four insurance classes during Beast Mode, which takes an extraordinary amount of time and effort.
- My back went out at one point, laying me up for about a week...but not my word count.
- I compiled the finished books into an omnibus called the *Beast Mode Collection* that I offered as a limited edition directly on my website.

I don't share my results to brag, but to show you what is possible when you pour your entire soul into a challenge. I would have never achieved these results in 2014 when I started publishing. But I've come far enough that I have a handle on craft, productivity, time management, and the emotional aspect of being a writer. Many writers would get trapped in their own heads during a challenge like this, especially if they did it in public. They'd be too worried about failing publicly. Me? I don't care. I win whether I lose or fail, and that mindset is one of my hidden secrets to success.

For me, a challenge is just a game. It exists for me to test my limits and break past barriers I wasn't aware were there. It's fun entertainment for me, fun entertainment for my audience, and I share transparently whether I win or lose. Then I take the lessons I learn, roll them into my next project, and keep leveling up.

The funny part? There's always someone better than you. Sure, I wrote seven books in three months, which is more than some authors write in several *years*...but right after I finished the challenge, long-time prolific author Dean Wesley Smith announced that he was going to "write his age"—publish 70 books in an entire year. Yes, you read that correctly. I have a sneaking suspicion that Dean will make my Beast Mode look like the amateur hour at a comedy club. That's master craftsmanship at a completely different level, especially because he's doing it with novels.

No matter how hard you push yourself, there are always new levels of learning.

THE PRICE OF BEAST MODE

I paid a hidden price for my Beast Mode challenge: focusing only on writing for 90 days meant that I neglected marketing and other areas of my business.

I knew this would happen, but I underestimated the extent to which it would hurt.

After all, I'm a part-time writer. I have to spend my time deliberately. Most days, I have to decide between writing and marketing. I can survive a week without marketing, but three months is problematic.

Some of my Amazon Ads switched off without me realizing it for a few days, resulting in lost income. My email inbox grew out of control and emails went unanswered. I missed sales opportunities, and at least one direct sales order of about $100 because the lead went cold.

I'm not complaining. I put myself in this situation. But when I think about other authors who do the same thing for months if not years, it could be a major reason why people don't sell more books.

For most of us, writing is safe. It's comfortable. Marketing is hard. When we do less of it, we make less money.

I do very little marketing in my business, and that's by design. I've managed to do pretty well for myself by focusing on organic growth and portfolio volume. It's not a strategy for the faint of heart. But when I stopped doing the little marketing I usually do, it hurt for a while.

The good news is that the seven books I wrote during Beast Mode started generating income immediately, so in a way, the sacrifice was worth it because I more than doubled the size of my nonfiction portfolio. But this chapter is a reminder that we pay a price for every decision we make in the writing life. Not all decisions have such happy consequences.

FICTIONALIZING THE REAL WORLD

I like to take chances when I write. For most of my books, I begin with an idea that can roughly be described as "this will either be awesome or it will end in flames." That's the only qualification for every book I've ever written. The result is that I have some books that don't "hit," but the ones that do usually do pretty well.

In the early days of my YouTube channel, I offered a lead magnet for my email newsletter called "The Indie Author Roadmap." I outlined the different things that an author needs to learn to start their writing business. It had a decent conversion rate, driving around 100 signups one year, maybe more. That's a low number by most marketing standards, but pretty good if you consider that I did almost nothing to promote it.

Over time, the lead magnet became outdated, so I retired it.

This year, I mentioned it in a video and people in my audience said they wanted to see me bring it back. There's no shortage of things to learn, and the landscape has changed a lot since 2015.

I played around with the idea of updating the PDF and making it available to people for free, but as I combed through it,

I realized that a PDF full of bullet points was...boring. It worked in 2015, but I owed a better product to my audience in 2020.

One day, I had a weird idea: what if I took all of the things that a writer needs to learn to be successful and turned them into fictional vacation destinations? What would the locales be like? What if I could reimagine the writing world as a fictional world?

The result was The Indie Author Atlas: Your Guide to the Five Continents of the Writing World. It's written in the style of a *Lonely Planet* travel guide with an imaginative and humorous tone.

Since the writing life can overwhelm you with all the things you have to learn, I tried to make the act of learning fun.

Each continent represents an area of the writing life: The Commonwealth of Craft, Marketstan, the twin utopias of Technology and Data, the Sacred Lands of Distribution, and the Kingdom of Business. Each continent has many cities and tourist attractions within, each with their own chapter that suggests what you need to learn without beating you over the head about it. I used a fictional narrative to frame concepts in ways that you might not think about.

For example, the first place in the Commonwealth of Craft you visit is the Dreadwood Nature Preserve, a shadowy woodscape where your psychological shadow tries to ruin your vacation. It's hardly a vacation destination, but I can't think of a better way to illustrate how fear and self-doubt ruin our travels in this beautiful writing world.

Once you escape from Dreadwood, you arrive at the Learning Lodge, a western-style lodge just outside the dangerous woods built by an elderly couple who want to help writers learn. The lodge is a place of refuge and rest, and while there, you learn "what you need to learn."

With the book, I also had the idea to commission custom

illustrated maps of each of the continents. I hired a designer whose style I loved, and she helped me take the atlas to the next level. This was a gigantic financial risk, but I believed it was worth it to realize my vision.

It's too soon to report on sales, so we'll see how the book does. But regardless of the result, I created a piece of art that I am proud of.

TRANSFORMING THE EMOTIONAL PROBLEMS OF THE WRITING WORLD INTO MONSTERS

I had another idea for a writing book that fell into the "this will either be awesome or will end in flames" territory.

I talk frequently about fear, self-doubt, and other emotional challenges in the writing life. Sometimes battling them is like battling a monster that shows up unexpectedly during a writing session.

This was right around the time I was writing *The Indie Author Atlas*, and I thought, "What if I took the emotional problems of the writing world, turned them into mythical beasts, and taught writers how to slay them?"

The result was The Indie Author Bestiary: An Epic Quest Against the Beasts of the Writing World. It is inspired by medieval bestiaries and *Shadow of the Colossus* (a classic PlayStation game).

I studied medieval bestiaries for structure and I drew from Middle Age lore. The book features 21 beasts, which symbolizes perfection and maturity in Christianity.

But unlike a typical bestiary, which explains the existence of the beast through a folk tale, I made this one a narrative told through the second person, but with a twist...

You are a knight wandering in the dangerous writing world. In the first chapter, you encounter Michael La Ronn, who is also an elder, more experienced knight. Michael takes you in and trains you how to fight. Then something dastardly happens, and you and Michael ride off to do battle with the 21 beasts who have gathered at a sinister tower. A beast resides on each story of the tower, and you and Michael climb and fight your way to the top.

You do battle with fear, self-doubt, the inferiority complex, and more—all envisioned as nightmarish, cunning monsters whose only purpose is to destroy you. The battles are equally physical and psychological.

Technically, Michael narrates the story, speaking to you, the hero. So when Michael is around, he handles the narrative. But at times, he exits the stage, and the narrative shifts to pure second person POV.

The book was the most technically complicated nonfiction I've ever written. I followed my subconscious, even though it was not easy. How do you handle things like the five senses when another character is telling the story, but the viewpoint is through the second person POV? How do you handle narrative shifts? How do you handle descriptions of things?

The book was great fun. Not only was it entertaining to write myself into a book for a change, it was challenging to push the boundaries of my storytelling ability. I hope others find the book entertaining and instructive.

I even commissioned a medieval self-portrait of myself as a knight with a dragon companion. I had way too much fun producing this book.

TURNING A PODCAST INTO A BOOK

Since July 2019, I have hosted a podcast called "Writing Tip of the Day." Every Monday through Friday, I share a writing tip in five minutes or less.

I started the show primarily as an Amazon Alexa Flash Briefing because I wanted to be an early mover in the smart speaker market. The show receives a modest amount of downloads every day, though not anything spectacular by any means. But the listeners who love it *really* love it because it's no-frills, no bullshit, and you can binge it. A lot of people start their workday with it.

I also syndicate the show to podcast networks such as Apple, Stitcher, and Spotify.

I had an idea to take the first year of the show and repurpose it into a book to bring in more listeners to the show. I called it the 250+ Writing Tips series.

I took the tips and reimagined them onto the written page. It would have been easy to use audio transcripts of the show, but that's the cheap and lazy way to do it. I wrote every chapter myself, often expanding on the original tip and adding even more value.

The book consists of short chapters organized by different areas of the writing life. The series hook is that it's the most comprehensive writing omnibus on the market.

When I'm done with the second year of Writing Tip of the Day, I will spin those tips in Volume 2, and so on.

Imagine an omnibus called 1000+ *Writing Tips*, full of unique and interesting tips you won't find anywhere else. I engineered the series to have "one-click" potential—if someone likes the first book, they'll buy the whole series in one click.

So far, Volume 1 is available, but I believe the series has immense long-term potential. It'll take at least two or three years for me to see the return on the investment, but when I do, it will have been worth it.

Also, I probably won't continue "Writing Tip of the Day" forever. When I pull the podcast down in the future, it will be nice to have memorialized the content in book form.

THE AUDIOBOOK PRODUCTION PROBLEM

Earlier in the year, I recorded my first audiobook. It was a fantastic experience.

However, I am now suffering from the consequences of recording your own audiobook: it's extraordinarily time-consuming. Even with shortcuts.

I'm not complaining, though. Just explaining why.

Let's say that I have a four-hour audiobook.

I have to record the book, which takes around five to six hours since I make mistakes.

Then I have to edit the audio I recorded, which takes another five to six hours. This includes re-recording sentences here and there.

That's twelve hours to record a four-hour audiobook. And honestly, it takes more time than that when you factor in exporting the audio, uploading it, and dealing with QA issues.

To give you some context, it takes me approximately forty hours to write a novel. Therefore, an audiobook takes approximately a third of the time it would take me to write a novel. Consider that I can write around five to seven writing books per year and you can see the problem: I can't record audiobooks fast enough.

I've experimented with unusual ideas to solve this problem. The first is developing a "magic number" for length. If an audiobook is under the magic number, then I do everything myself. If it's above that number, I hire an engineer to do the editing and mastering so that I only have to do the recording. But that route has its problems, namely cost. The main reason I recorded my own audiobooks was because of the profit margin. Even if it takes twelve hours, there's no expense other than my time. Whatever I would pay an engineer is usually equivalent to what I'd pay a professional narrator. Economically and time-wise, it doesn't make sense.

The second idea is hiring a recording studio to help me record the book. But again, cost. And I'm not convinced that executing on the highest possible quality is worth it for a short audiobook. Readers are listening for the information. They don't care, as long as the audio quality is *good enough*. A thirty-hour audiobook? Different story. But most of my writing books are short.

I'm betting on the fact that audiobooks narrated by the author are a unique selling point. And I believe that. But I have to avoid making unwise decisions with my time.

So the verdict is that I will continue to record audiobooks, but I've accepted that my pace will be slower for a while.

ASSISTANT FOR A DAY

Writer's Digest asked me to speak at their Annual Writer's Digest Conference this year. What an honor to speak at the conference sponsored by the writing magazine I used to read as a kid!

The conference was virtual this year due to the pandemic. *Writer's Digest* hired a conference platform called Intrado to facilitate the speaker sessions. Intrado was like Zoom on steroids. Each speaker received their own dedicated audiovisual engineer as well as a *Writer's Digest* staff member on-call if needed.

Intrado had another feature that was cool in theory, but problematic in execution: a chat box as well as a question and answer box. The chat box needs no explanation—it existed solely for viewers to engage with each other during the chat.

However, the question and answer box were more complicated. Viewers could ask questions and then the questions would flow through to me while I was speaking. I could then approve questions and organize them based on high, medium, and low priority.

There was only one problem: I was expected to monitor the chat *and* manage the questions in real-time while I gave the talk.

Nope. Just thinking about that gives me chills even to this day. This was my biggest speaking engagement of the year and I was determined not to screw it up, especially since it was going to end up on YouTube.

So I hired a virtual assistant on Upwork for one day only. She only had three jobs:

- Monitor the chat and post links to my YouTube channel and the book I covered in the talk if people asked for them. (My experience with live events is that people join late and sometimes miss the opening of the talk, or they ask for links that you give—even if you repeat it multiple times.)
- Organize the viewer questions so that I could answer them when I arrived at the Q&A session at the end.
- Export the questions to a Word document for me so I could study them after the event and give me a report of what people said in the chat.

I needed her to do those things so I could focus on giving the talk. I also didn't want there to be awkwardness as I transitioned from the talk to the Q&A.

And guess what? Everything went smoothly! The assistant was phenomenal and she went above and beyond what I asked her to do.

Sure, I had to spend a portion of my speaker fee to pay her, but it was worth it. The talk went so well that it led to future opportunities to work with *Writer's Digest*, which is a win. Money well-spent, in my opinion.

AMNESIA MODE

I discussed previously the cost of my Beast Mode challenge. Since I neglected my marketing, I decided to make that my next challenge from November 1st to January 15th.

I called it "Amnesia Mode."

I pretended that I fell down and hit my head and forgot everything I knew about marketing.

What could I learn? What would change in my business if I approached every marketing concept again with the eyes of a newbie who knew nothing?

This challenge was far more balanced than Beast Mode, since I wrote books during it.

While the challenge is still ongoing at the time of this writing, it has been a hit with my audience. Many of the people who follow me are always looking for ways to sell more books and they appreciate transparency.

Every day on my blog, I share a lesson learned and a lesson executed.

A lesson learned is usually from a book I'm reading or marketing course I purchased.

A lesson executed is when I take action. I cover exactly what I did, play-by-play.

My hope is that Amnesia Mode will expand my mind to new opportunities, help me stay current with new marketing trends, and improve my sales.

If I improve my sales, others can follow what I did. If I don't, others will know what possibly didn't work, and why. Win-win.

I'll share the results of Amnesia Mode in the next volume of this series.

PITCHING FOR A TED TALK

I've always dreamt of giving a TED talk. It's a public speaker's paradise: you share your biggest idea in front of an enthusiastic, thoughtful crowd, and watch the idea spread all over the globe.

I watch TED Talks frequently. I even bought a couple books a few years ago about how to land and deliver one just in case I ever found myself in the position...

My understanding was that you had to know someone who knew someone in order to get selected. As such, I had written off the possibility of giving a talk until way into the future.

Imagine my surprise when I discovered on LinkedIn that TEDx was coming to Des Moines, Iowa where I live, and they were accepting applications for local speakers!

My head almost exploded. This was the opportunity of a lifetime.

So many thoughts raced through my mind.

"Can I apply?"

"*Should* I apply?"

"Would they even accept me?"

"I'm not credentialed or sophisticated enough to be a TED speaker."

"I don't fit the TED mold."

"What would I even talk about?"

I almost talked myself out of applying, honestly. I wasn't sure that they'd be interested in anything I had to say.

But then I realized that applying for a talk would be the ultimate test of my marketing skills at this point in time, especially since I was in the middle of my Amnesia Mode challenge. I would likely be an underdog in the applicant pool, so I'd have to create a pitch that was superior in every way.

The deadline was quickly approaching, so I gave myself an eight-hour deadline to come up with a talk and submit the application. No excuses, no procrastination. I would do it, be done, and move on with my life. Like going to the grocery store and buying toothpaste. That was the only way I could mentally address the task without dwelling on it and spending days or weeks preparing an idea.

I blocked four hours to think about the topic. I didn't want to get up on stage and talk about writing. That's too niche for TED audiences. When I think of TED talks, I imagine highly credible speakers talking about highly specific topics that have broad appeal. Writing a book doesn't fit that mold, so I had to think broader. I focused instead about being a creative. I found a topic from an old autoresponder I wrote that resonated with my audience, and I made that the basis for the talk. If selected, it might be the only talk that ever originated from an autoresponder.

Then I used a method that worked well for me in the past: the 3-Minute Rule by Brant Pinvidic. The gist of the method is that you start with an idea and follow a guided pattern to grow it into a pitch that is three minutes or less. It contains all the details the decision-makers need to know while also addressing their potential objections. This is the method that Pinvidic (a

TV executive) used to pitch some of the most famous shows on TV.

Developing the pitch took me about two hours.

With two hours left, it was time to fill out the application. I had to provide a three-sentence description of the talk as well as record a three- to five-minute video explaining the talk and why I wanted to do it.

Ironically, I made a pitch video that was exactly three minutes long using a mixture of Pinvidic's guidance, basic sales tactics such as a strong closing, and my prior YouTube experience. I filmed the audition on my DSLR in the same way that I record my YouTube videos, with good sound and lighting. I finished with about thirty minutes to spare.

We'll see what happens. If I land the talk, it will be purely because my pitch was on-point. I don't know anyone on the selection panel and they don't know me, so I don't have any connections to rely on. If I don't land it, who knows—maybe my pitch was ineffective or maybe the committee already had people picked out. It doesn't matter.

Regardless, I'm pretty proud that I applied. It was also great content for my community. I wrote about the experience in a newsletter, talked about it on *The Writer's Journey* podcast, and I dedicated this chapter to it!

A major weakness that a lot of writers have today is marketing themselves. I don't pretend to be good at it, but I'm willing to try and improve. The process of pitching a TED talk is really no different than pitching a short story to a literary magazine or a book to listeners during a podcast interview. The results may be different, but the steps are the same. It would be pretty cool to share the exact steps I followed if I land the talk. Maybe it could help a few folks.

BECOME A WORLD-CLASS MARKETER

LUNCHCLUB

So much in marketing is about relationships and your network.

I received an invitation to join Lunchclub.AI, a platform that uses artificial intelligence to match people together for networking meetings. You create a profile, tell the platform what type of people you're interested in meeting, link it with your calendar, and the next day, you receive email introductions with people you're going to meet. The platform handles the scheduling and the Zoom calls. All you have to do is show up and talk to people.

I was skeptical of the service at first, but now I'm one of its biggest fans.

In the first few weeks of the service, I talked to so many interesting people:

- An award-winning poet (a very *acclaimed* poet, actually)
- A money coach
- A freelance marketing director who works with big brands

- A yoga instructor who moonlights in using the power of AI to drive lifestyle design

All of the conversations were insanely interesting. I learned something from each person.

We just chatted about our careers and followed the conversation down interesting paths. Most of the conversations ended with a "feel free to reach out any time if you have questions about X." And that's fine, since that's how most networking conversations in real life end.

I don't have any expectations about Lunchclub, but maybe one day some of these connections I'm making will come in handy.

THE HOLY DUO OF MARKETING: THE BOOK DESCRIPTION AND OPENING CHAPTER

I was browsing Amazon for bestselling self-published books to see how their book descriptions were worded. I noticed something that seems obvious now, but somehow, I missed it for years.

I looked at books with at least 100 reviews. Without exception for the dozen or so books I studied, if you read the book description, it matches the first page of the story. The book description serves as a primer. The first page delivers.

For example, the book description might say "Now I have to figure out why a vampire is in my backyard trying to kill me." The first page of the book will be the hero in their backyard, fighting a vampire.

It's helpful to think of the book description and the opening chapter as an interlocking unit. What one starts, the other finishes.

REPURPOSED SPEAKING ENGAGEMENTS

I was invited to several speaking engagements this year. Due to the pandemic, the events were cancelled in-person and moved online. This meant that I either had to pre-record a video of my speech or livestream it.

In each case, I asked if the venue planned to upload the speeches to YouTube. One of them told me no. No????!!

Opportunity, opportunity, opportunity!

They told me I was welcome to upload the talk to my channel after the event was over. I told them I'd give them 60 days as a courtesy. Additionally, the speaking agreement does not take the copyright or place any limitations on what I can do with the talk, so the copyright is mine, baby!

(See, this is why it pays to understand copyright. I was able to anticipate this before signing the contract.)

The venue got (hopefully) a good talk from me.

I got to repurpose the content and post to my YouTube channel, which is quality content for my audience. YouTube also favors longer videos, so the ad revenue is better. It also boosts my credibility.

Everyone wins.

This is why I'm always careful to ask about repurposing the talk before I do the event.

CUSTOMER SERVICE IS A CONSCIOUSNESS

I listened to a great podcast interview where the interviewee was talking about her first job as a waitress. She described how she learned to tell what customers wanted, and how waitressing is the embodiment of the golden rule: treat others how *they* want to be treated.

For example, some patrons don't want to chat with a waitress. They just want to eat. Other patrons are a little *too* chatty. It's the waitress's job to figure out what each person wants and balance their interests accordingly.

She then said something that clicked with me: "Customer service is a consciousness."

Some people have that consciousness, and others don't. For example, an Internet tech came to my house once to help me with a bad Wi-Fi signal. We ended up making small talk, and he gave me some extra tips on how to maintain a good signal. This was the third time the Internet company had been at my house in six months. The other techs tried to fix the problem as soon as they could and didn't explain very much to me. This guy took the time to help and teach me to fix the problem myself so that I didn't have to call again. He also told me that one of his favorite parts about the job was working with the elderly. He said that it was time-consuming working with them, but they were always grateful for the help.

That's the customer service "consciousness." The tech had it.

Let me give you an example of someone who didn't have it. I upgraded my cell phone, an ordeal that took three hours because I had to buy and activate new phones for me, my wife, *and* my in-laws. The sales representative at the store was a young woman who just graduated high school. She was friendly enough, and we didn't have any problems in the store.

The next day, I received an unexpected charge on my bill. I couldn't figure out what it was, so I called the corporate headquarters. They told me that the "discount" the sales representative promised me wasn't actually a discount. I had to pay in full first and then it would post to my account in 90 days (or something like that—I'm still not sure I understood what the hell they told me). Really? Why didn't the sales representative tell me that when I was in the store? She had to have known as this is a routine sale the store runs, and she told me she had been working there for about two years. She didn't have the customer service consciousness. A better salesperson would have explained the billing problem in the store; otherwise, there's a high chance customers will return angry, and that's bad for business.

In the customer service world, this is called the "first time final" problem. Companies grade their representatives on how well they handled an encounter by gauging if the customer has to call back within a certain time period. Again, this is part of the consciousness.

What does this have to do with writers?

Whether you like it or not, you're in the customer service business.

Customer service needs arise in the following areas of the writing life:

- Prospective readers want to know which book in a series they should read first, or which *series* to read first. Your website had better offer that information; if not, readers will email you to ask the question directly, or they'll find another author who makes the buying process easier for them.
- When readers buy your book directly and need to sideload it onto their device.
- When readers email you with a question.
- When readers mention you on social media.

Those are just a few. There are more. When readers engage, are you ready?

Think of customer service as occurring in three phases: needs the customer has before they become a customer, needs the customer has when they're using your product, and needs when something goes wrong.

How are you serving your readers, and how can you develop the customer service "consciousness"?

WE KNOW WHY YOU'RE HERE

When I upgraded my phone this year, the cell phone store didn't have a good selection of accessories.

When I got home, I did a quick Internet search, and I stumbled across a well-known company that is known for making quality accessories for mobile phones.

When I clicked on the home page, the first thing on the top of the page was the newest iPhone and an assortment of accessories, with language that said something like "Looking for a case for your shiny new phone?"

Wow. That's some killer salesmanship!

They knew exactly why I was there and they read my mind; they knew that my cell phone store didn't have a good selection, and they capitalized on that.

Did I buy from their website? You betcha.

I thought about how I could accomplish something like this in my writing business. When done wrong, this sort of thing can be obnoxious.

An easy idea was to do it after speaking events, where I send people to a landing page on my site with the logo of the event and a headline that calls back to something I said in the talk. I'd offer one of my books on sale with a coupon code if they buy directly from me. I might also curate content from my YouTube channel or podcast that complements my talk and design the page in a simple but attractive layout.

Just an idea, but something I'd like to try in the future.

UPDATING BACK MATTER

I discovered an inconsistency in the back matter of my writing books.

One book had a sample of the next book in the series. Another had a buy link to the next book in the series. One didn't have a call to action at all!

Not good.

I standardized my back matter so that the elements appear in the same order every time.

I created a page called "Read Next" that has the cover of the next book in the series, some sales copy, and a link.

This way, no matter what book you're reading from me, the ending experience is the same.

I'm paying special attention to the interior consistency of my books. Long-term, I want readers to have the same general experience from cover to cover, no matter what book they're reading.

THE MARKETING METRICS THAT MATTER

Marketing is all about metrics and analytics. You can drown in numbers if you're not careful, and it's easy to focus on numbers that don't actually drive growth.

What are the key performance indicators (KPIs) for an author? In other words, if you filtered everything down to a few key numbers that tell you how your business is performing, what would they be?

In the previous volume, I listed my sales metrics. I've updated them. Here they are:

- **Net Units Sold**: The total number of books I have sold, with refunds subtracted.
- **Income**: How much money I make from my books and other revenue sources.
- **Revenue Stream Mix**: A breakdown of how much I make across different retailers, geographies, and across different channels such as fiction versus nonfiction.

- **Expenses**: How much money I have spent in the business.
- **Yearly Cost**: How much it costs per year to run the business.
- **Profit**: Revenue minus expenses.
- **Leverage Ratio**: How well-funded the business is. How much money is in the bank account versus the yearly cost? If I have $100 in the bank account and it costs $1000 to run the business, that's a leverage ratio of 0.10 (100 divided by 1000), which is pretty bad. I'm too leveraged and it means I have to borrow from my personal savings to pay expenses. On the other hand, if I have $1200 in the bank and it costs $1000 to run the business for the next year, that's a leverage ratio of 1.2 (1200 divided by 1000), which is better. It means that if something unforeseen happened, I'd have enough cash on-hand to last me the next year, plus a little extra. The higher the leverage ratio, the better.

I can also view the metrics above:

- Year over year or month or over month
- For any given time period

Over the years, I've stopped tracking a lot of marketing metrics. Numbers like website analytics, link tracking, number of reviews, and review averages don't tell me very much about the vitality of the business.

Ultimately, it boils down to how much money is coming in, how much money is going out, which products are driving the growth, which expenses are driving your spending, and how insulated the business is from shock.

I settled on these numbers this quarter because I am planning on building a visual dashboard that shows me this data automatically.

VIDEO TRAILER ADVERTISING A COURSE

I happened upon a YouTube channel for writers. The YouTuber sold writing craft courses. She created a one-minute trailer for each course, explaining what the course was, why it was important, and an intriguing example tip that demonstrated what you would learn.

The trailers were a free and smart way to promote the courses. While the videos didn't have many views, that wasn't the point. The YouTuber made the videos to make prospective buyers (me) *aware* that the course existed. I ended up buying one of them because it covered something I had been wanting to learn for a long time. If it hadn't been for the video, I might have missed it.

I made a mental note of the technique so I could try it when I create my next course.

FACEBOOK LESSON LEARNED

In the last volume, I wrote about a sales failure involving Facebook and a delayed response on my part that cost me a big sale. I wrote about how I fixed the problem so it wouldn't happen.

Sure enough, someone else messaged me on Facebook with a basic question. I received an immediate notification and responded right away. The reader then started a conversation with me and asked if I would be willing to sell them signed paperbacks of my *Galaxy Mavericks* series. Galaxy Mavericks is nine books with an average paperback price of $10. Do the math.

KA-CHING!

That's how you fix problems on your platform and stop sales from leaking through. A simple two-minute fix on Facebook a few months ago made all the difference here.

DIRECT SALES INTEGRATION

I finally got around to implementing direct ebook sales on authorlevelup.com.

I used to have it, but I wasn't happy with the provider, so I removed the option. Plus, it didn't sell well anyway.

I integrated with Payhip, which is a great service that makes it easy for readers to buy quickly. You can also do coupon codes.

Within 48 hours of integrating direct sales onto my website, I started seeing sales. Nothing substantial, but small revenue streams add up into mighty rivers over time.

I'll eventually install Payhip on michaellaronn.com too, but I'm waiting to see if there are any issues with the service. So far, it's working well.

At the end of my Beast Mode challenge, I packaged all the books I wrote into a single book and sold it only on my website, which helped bring in some additional income that I wasn't expecting.

Now I need to figure out how to do direct audio and paper-back sales. There are two providers I am sourcing right now, but I don't like that you can't sell ebooks, audiobooks, and paperbacks all from one retailer. You can *in theory*, but it's not the best customer experience right now. I'll discuss this later in the book.

P.A.S.T.O.R-ING YOUR CUSTOMERS

I read *Copy That Sells* by Ray Edwards. Ray is an acclaimed copywriter who has worked with many big-name clients.

I've read a lot of copywriting books, but Ray's book clicked with me. Suddenly I understood copywriting on a completely different level.

A major takeaway from the book was Ray's P.A.S.T.O.R method of copywriting, a technique he uses to write sales letters that "shepherds" prospective customers from awareness to paying customer. Through the method, you focus on the following elements:

Focus on the **p**erson, pain, problem.

Amplify the problem.

Tell the **s**tory of the target person, explain the solution and the system they can follow.

Tell the story of **t**ransformation and use testimonials.

Make an **o**ffer.

Anticipate the customer's **r**esponse to the offer.

Do those things, and you will increase your chance of pastoring them into your flock.

I'll admit that Ray's method wasn't helpful for fiction marketing, but I found it invaluable for email newsletters and other sales techniques. It's a smart way of thinking about your customers.

LIFE'S A SQUEEZE

I read a copywriting book by an advertising legend. At the end of the book, there was a call to action to download a special offer.

I clicked the link and it took me to an outdated squeeze page that made me question if the author still maintained it. (A squeeze page is a landing page intended solely to convince visitors to take an action, such as joining a mailing list.)

In fact, the page was *so* out-of-touch that I decided not to download the offer.

I immediately checked my squeeze pages to see how they'd aged. I made some minor tweaks to them that should make them timeless.

Definitely not a mistake I want to make. This particular writer should have known better.

BECOME A TECHNOLOGY-DRIVEN WRITER

TECHNOLOGY IS THE KEY

When I talk about technology, I often hear people say that it's too complicated or that they don't have time to learn. After all, so many of us are just focused on writing next book.

I get it.

And I would understand resistance even more if people had to pay big money to download new apps and services to accomplish the kind of automation I am referring to.

But almost all of the tools we can use to automate portions of our writing business *are already on our computers*. We just aren't aware of them, or don't know how to use them to their true potential.

So much technology is literally at our fingertips.

There's a great movie called *Defending Your Life* with Albert Brooks. In one scene, the hero goes to the afterlife, where he meets several people, each of whom has unlocked more percentage of their brain than the average person. Technology is like that—you can unlock more of your computer's processing power, get more value out of the apps and services you already use, all at little or no cost.

My ultimate goal is to create a writing business that practically runs itself. I'd like to spend as little time as possible doing nonessential tasks.

The more time I spend writing and marketing and the less time I spend doing clerical tasks the better. Using automation to help me with that directly translates into revenue; for many of the tasks I am automating, most people would either not do them or hire an assistant at an expensive hourly rate.

Let's just say for the sake of easy math that I hired an assistant full-time to do clerical tasks for me without any automation. And let's say that it's a good assistant, commanding at least $30/hour or more.

That's $1,200 per week, or around $60,000 per year.

For easy math, let's say that I could automate around 50% of the tasks that the assistant could do. That cuts my costs down to $600 per week, or about $30,000 per year. I can then take that $30,000 per year I saved and invest in more activities that will bring in money. For example, my Amazon Ads are very profitable. What if I took that extra $30,000, put it into ads and turned it into $50,000?

Or what if I could use that extra income to pay off my house and therefore reduce hardship when my income decreases?

Or invest in a startup in the writing space? Or keep it in the bank for a rainy day?

Or...?

The margin between what I can automate versus outsource is what I call the "margin of opportunity." It will allow me to do things that others can't. It's a strategic advantage.

Combine the "margin of opportunity" with:

- A well-capitalized business with enough in savings to deal with surprises;
- A low overhead expense load; and

- A *profit* that pays a living wage;

And you have a recipe for amazing innovation and growth.

Now that I *really* have your attention, I repeat: you can take steps to achieve this today using the *tools that are already on your computer.*

Don't believe me?

Microsoft Excel allows you to automate data entry and data analysis.

Microsoft Word also offers macros, and you can use free macros off the Internet to help you catch more spelling and grammar errors than its spell checker can.

Microsoft Powershell, Applescripts, and Apple Automator allow you to automate routine tasks on your computer.

Programs like Apple Time Machine allow you to back up your work automatically.

Your email client allows you create filters or email rules to manage the flow of your emails.

Free apps like Calendly allow people to grab time on your calendar, eliminating "scheduling" emails between you and another person.

Formatting apps such as Vellum allow you to create better formatted books in less time.

Some writing apps allow direct integration with WordPress so you can blog directly from your app without having to sign in to WordPress.

Spell checker apps like ProWritingAid and Grammarly check your manuscript for additional spelling errors that you might have otherwise missed.

Social media scheduling apps allow you to schedule posting content well into the future. Almost all of them have free plans that are more than enough for most authors.

Again, all of this is free. What would your writing business look like if you optimized your time accordingly? How much time and money would you save, and could you invest that time and money back into your business in ways that support your mission and drive growth?

ZAPIER IS FOR AUTOMATION

Zapier is a web service that helps you automate routine tasks by linking other web services together.

For example, if you have a Mailchimp mailing list, you might want to download your subscriber information into a spreadsheet on Google Sheets. You can create an automation task so that every time you receive a new subscriber, Zapier will download that information into Google Sheets. You never have to get involved other than to make sure that the automation is working.

I've been aware of Zapier for a while, but I didn't understand how powerful it was until now.

I'm playing around with a few ideas to help me automate areas of the business that are less essential.

For example, bookkeeping. It's necessary, but it's not an "essential" task that *I* should be doing. I have an accountant who handles that for me, but he uses Quickbooks, which I despise because it doesn't offer the flexibility that I prefer when I'm digging through my expenses. I like to categorize my expenses based on more obvious terms, such as editing, marketing, continuing education, and so on.

My idea is to create a Frankenstein automation sequence that follows these steps:

- In Gmail, create filters for every expense receipt I receive so that new expenses get marked as "read" and moved into a dedicated folder.
- Once an expense receipt hits my inbox, Gmail moves the receipt into the folder.
- Zapier (which is connected to Gmail) then identifies the expense type and "parses" the email, looking for the date, company name, item name (if possible), and the price.
- Zapier then passes the "parsed" data fields to Google Sheets, where I have a spreadsheet that corresponds with the data fields, as well as a category column with an IF formula that tags each expense as a certain category depending on what the data says.
- Zapier moves the original email into another folder that lets me know that the expense was parsed.
- Once per month, a calendar reminder hits my inbox. I go to Google Sheets, verify the expenses, and fix any data that didn't pass through correctly. Inevitably, there will be some issues here and there.

I currently spend around one hour to 90 minutes preparing my expenses each month. I already set up Gmail filters a few months ago as part of a separate project, so that's done. I just need to create the "zaps" in Zapier, which would take me about 30 minutes to configure.

I believe that automating this activity would save me around 40 to 80 minutes each month. That means I would reduce my

time spend to around 10 to 20 minutes. That's the very defini-
tion of efficiency because I can spend the time I save doing other
things in the business that drive revenue and growth.

FOLLOW-UP ON PERSONAL THANK YOU VIDEOS

In Volume 1 of this series, I wrote how I started using the app Bonjoro to send personal thank you videos to people who buy my courses.

I implemented direct ebook sales on my website this quarter, and I added thank you videos into the workflow when someone buys a book directly from me.

I received the following responses from readers:

"THANKS so much for the personalized 'thank you' video!

"I was pleasantly shocked to hear my name (yes, you pronounced it correctly--LOL) along with your offer to answer questions about the material in your book collection.

"What a classy thing to do! I truly appreciate it and I'll be sure to reach out if I have any questions."

Just a sign that the technique works, and when it does, it works amazingly well.

I still don't advertise that I do this except for writing about it in the *Indie Author Confidential* series. It's a neat little surprise.

I checked my Bonjoro dashboard for analytics because I was curious what kind of data they provide. Of all the video messages I've sent:

- 93% were opened
- 100% of the opened messages were watched
- 43% replied

Solid numbers. It's good to know that the messages aren't going into people's spam filters and that people aren't having any trouble watching the videos.

I'll keep doing this until it becomes logistically impossible. And even then, I may keep doing it in some capacity.

MORE EXCEL ADVENTURES

I took a new job that challenged me in ways I've never been challenged before. It involves a *lot* of data and analytics, to the point where I have to be a numbers person. That's a scary proposition for someone who struggles with basic arithmetic and has no statistical background. But hey, I'm up to the challenge. It's good for me, and I can port the lessons I learn into my writing business, so it's a win-win.

The more time I spend in Microsoft Excel, the more I believe it is the most powerful application ever created. No other application I can think of even comes close to the sheer power and breadth of services that Excel provides. Not by a long shot.

However, Excel has a marketing problem. Too many people (myself included) think it's an app for numbers people. It certainly does have functions that automate math, but it's not a numbers app at its core.

Excel is a *logic* application. It offers tools you think critically about problems and answer questions you have about your data. "Numbers" are only a small part of the experience.

I actually think a lot of writers who are scared of Excel

could do pretty well at it if there were better resources out there on how to use Excel for your writing business. Excel is ultimately about using logic to think critically—writers do that every day with their stories. We're good problem solvers.

But Excel and (most) writers don't mix. Almost every writer I've ever talked to is terrified of it.

Anyway, I gained experience with the following features that I believe could be game-changers for writers.

Pivot tables are essential Excel learning. I read an article online that said it is estimated 90% of Excel users don't know how to use them. Considering I didn't know how to use one until about six months ago, and almost no one I know even knows what they are, I consider that an accurate statement. They're not hard to learn, but you do have to watch a few YouTube videos and play around with them for a while before it clicks.

I use pivot tables and pivot charts to help me gain insights into my sales. I also use them to help me cut through the noise of certain reports. For example, my AMS Ad search terms report is a pain to read. Put it into a pivot table and it becomes instantly more readable.

Believe it or not, you can throw your monthly sales reports into pivot tables too.

I learned a ton of other things about Excel in doing this new job. I'd bore you if I shared them, but it got me thinking about a way to make Excel easier for writers so they could unlock some more of the benefits.

FIXED MY INTERNET CONNECTION

In Volume 2 of this series, I recounted how my second interview with Joanna Penn for "The Creative Penn Podcast" went awry because my WiFi decided to go on vacation when we started recording. I swore that this would never happen again, so I wanted to follow up on my progress.

I hired an electrician to install ethernet ports in my studio so that I can connect my computer to hard Internet when I'm working from home and doing speaking interviews. This way, I (hopefully) will not have to worry about dropped connections.

I also had the Internet company come over and fix some things at the house that were causing signal issues. I should be all set now.

This is a win because it improves my professionalism. Yet, this professionalism is invisible. No one ever thinks "I'm glad Michael has a good Internet connection" when they're interviewing me. But they think the opposite the moment my signal drops. My goal is to never have a dropped signal ever again with any speaking engagement. Will that be possible? Probably not—things always happen outside of my control, but at least I know I'm doing all I can on my end.

The work in my studio was also tax-deductible, so another win.

Since installing the ethernet ports, I have done approximately seven podcast interviews and three speaking engagements. No signal drops for any of them.

I'd call that a huge level up.

TYPO REPORTER

My friend Kevin Tumlinson has a cool way to catch typos in his work. In the back matter of his books, he includes a link to a page that encourages readers to contact him if they find a typo. The page includes a form that readers fill out to help him identify the error.

He also thanks readers who catch typos in his future books on the acknowledgments page.

This is a smart idea if you're on a budget but want some additional support with proofreading. It's smart, even if you hire multiple editors. While not something I plan to implement personally, I wanted to pass the idea along.

DAILY PROMPT

I received an email from the developer of an iOS app for writers called Daily Prompt. The app is designed to help writers beat writer's block by giving them daily inspiration and writing prompts. I featured the app on my YouTube channel.

Each day, the developer curates beautiful and thought-provoking images that are designed to stimulate your imagination. There are also daily written prompts.

I love the idea. It reminds me ten years ago when I was a beginning writer and a friend and I would come up with writing prompts each week to write stories to. Many weeks, we struggled with ideas. An app like this would have been great for that.

Daily Prompt is well-designed with a noble purpose. But most importantly, it offers a free version and is quite affordable. I can't think of a better way to use technology to solve an age-old problem.

SALES COPY BUILDER

One of my biggest problems with book descriptions is that I wait until the last minute to write them. As a result, they sometimes read like afterthoughts, which hurts my sales and creates rework for me later. Sometimes the descriptions are decent; other times they're terrible. I don't like that inconsistency. I want to create a description that is the same level of quality every time—preferably one that converts!

Another problem I have with book descriptions is that I write them so infrequently that I forget the best copywriting methods. Even if I publish seven books in a year, that's only seven days out of the year that I'm writing a book description, which isn't enough to build muscle memory quickly.

I need a structure that can help me remember the steps.

During my Amnesia Mode challenge, I reread books by authors whose methods are most popular for fiction: Bryan Cohen, Libbie Hawker, Dean Wesley Smith, and a few others.

I created a simple spreadsheet that I call my "Sales Copy Builder." It helps me snap the different elements of book descriptions together like LEGOs so I can build high-converting book descriptions in less time, with no consistency gaps.

Here's a screenshot of what this looks like for fiction:

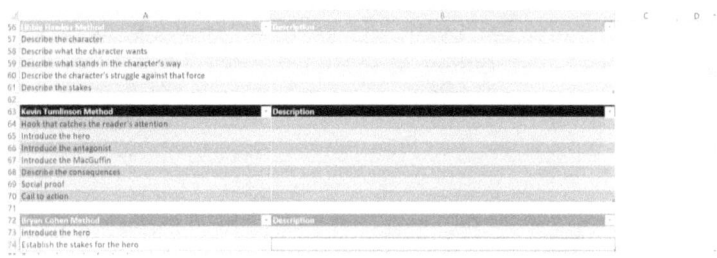

I broke each method into a series of steps, with each step representing a paragraph in Column A. In Column B, I write my book description. When I'm done, I simply copy all the cells in Column B and they copy over like magic into wherever I need them to go. When I'm done, I created a quick macro that erases all the content with the click of a button.

Here's what this looks like for nonfiction:

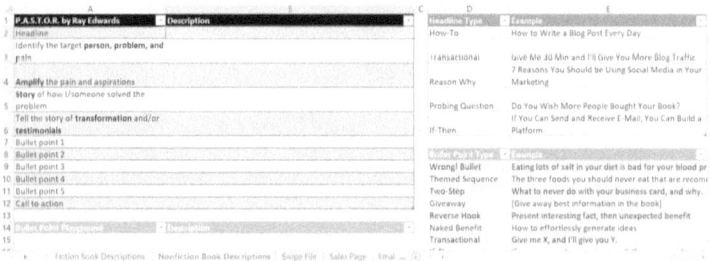

Nonfiction is different. In this screenshot, I have Ray Edwards's method laid out, but I also have some help documentation on the right to jog my memory. It's easy to forget that there are different types of headlines and even bullet points, for example. It's helpful to have that information on-hand in the same screen so I can refer to it.

This spreadsheet took me 45 minutes to create and it has

been a game changer. It improved my book descriptions overnight—not only were they more consistent, they didn't have anything missing. Even better, I can use the tool to write *several different book descriptions* at the same time! Then I can pick and choose lines that work best.

I also have a tab for email newsletters, since I write those monthly.

I also included a tab for a swipe file. I have collected clever marketing phrases and "money words" over the years, so I dumped them onto this tab so I can pull it up if I need some inspiration.

In my opinion, this is a perfect albeit unusual use case of how you can use existing apps and technology on your computer to help you execute better.

BROKEN WEBSITE

Once or twice a year, an element on my website breaks. Because I patrol my website properties so infrequently, I may not find out about the break until some time has passed.

Recently, a reader wrote me to tell me that my book pages were broken. I found the issue and fixed it, but I have no idea how long my website was malfunctioning, and that's scary.

Every time this happens, I tell myself I need a new website, but I can usually fix the issue to where it doesn't happen again. It's one of the downsides to WordPress. I minimize my plugins, but even then I have problems.

I set a reminder to patrol my website once every other month to catch errors earlier. I don't like to do that. A website should run itself with minimal interaction if needed.

But I do need a new website, which brings me to the next chapter...

PREPARING FOR A NEW WEBSITE

I need a new website, but I've been putting it off. I'll probably keep putting it off for a few more years. The only problem with that is that it will be more expensive the longer I wait.

I've published over 50 books. Each book has its own dedicated page on my sites. That's at least 50 pages that I would have to populate on a new website, or pay someone to do for me. Very, very expensive.

I also need better functionality on my site, as it has fallen behind the times. I've done all the little tweaks I can do at this point.

The nice part about author websites is that readers don't really care what they look like; they just care about finding the books they care about, and maybe learning a little about you in the process. So no one is going to come to my house and verbally berate me because my website is a little outdated.

However, this has given me the opportunity to think carefully about how I want to design my next website, and what types of functionality I want to have on it.

My first wishlist item is a professional design that suits my brand. I'm also desperate for a better sales experience. I need my website to be a "consummate salesperson," selling books at an even higher converting rate than it does now, all while I sleep.

My second wishlist item is to be up-to-date with all the latest web standards.

My third wishlist item is integration with a SQL server to solve the book page problem. I'd like to maintain a server that stores "one version of the truth"—all of my book metadata such as title, book description, book cover, links to retailers, and so on. This server would integrate with the website and communicate with it whenever I have a new change. For example, if I publish a new book, I'd update the SQL server, and then, within minutes, I'd have a new page on my site with all of the book's metadata laid out in accordance with how my designer designed the book pages to look. This way, all the book pages have a consistent look and feel, are always up-to-date, require zero maintenance, and could handle any amount of books I throw at it. While this might take some time and money for a programmer to create, it would save me time and maintenance costs over the life of the website.

My fourth wishlist item is smoother integration for eCommerce so I can create a better buying experience for readers who wish to purchase books from me directly.

My fifth wishlist item is a tool that can get the right book to the right readers at the right time. I have a simple tool on michaellaronn.com called Book Wizard. Book Wizard asks site users a series of questions and then recommends a book based on their answers. I envision something like this but on steroids. Ideally, it might even recommend books to a user based on their demographics or where they are coming from. Ideally, I would have back-end analytics that tell me which of my books are getting recommended most often and which ones are receiving clicks.

My sixth wishlist item is some kind of "break" detection. I want a notification when my website is not operating as intended. I also want a monthly report of broken links. I shouldn't have to find out from one of my readers that the site is broken or not functioning properly.

And lastly, I need to remain cognizant of emerging technology like AI-narrated audiobooks, cryptocurrencies, audiobook direct sales and delivery, artificial intelligence, and so much more. Those will play a prominent role in the future of author websites too.

At a minimum, even if I can't achieve *all* of these wishlist items, I need a website that is flexible enough to accommodate them in the future.

Will this be expensive? Yes...which is why I'm putting it off...

But if I can pull it off and execute it on a high level, it'll pay for itself over a few years.

In the meantime, I'll keep dreaming and saving.

BOOK BRUSH COVER DESIGNER

Book Brush is a web-based service that allows you to create professional marketing graphics for your book without having to use Photoshop.

Book Brush just released a new feature in their app suite called the Cover Designer. You can now design book covers in the app for ebook, paperback, and audio.

I've featured Book Brush on my YouTube channel, and I've done private webinars with them for my audience. I'm a big fan of the tool and I want more people to know about it.

The cover designer is a game changer. It allows authors who previously couldn't design their covers to do so with a small learning curve compared to Photoshop. The best part about it is that you can design a paperback and audio cover with no hassle. Just click a button and it automatically sets up the proper dimensions.

As they keep adding functionality, Book Brush could become the watershed tool that finally allows authors to create professional book covers at a fraction of the cost and in a fraction of the time. Is it a replacement for a cover designer? Probably not, but if you're tight on money, it's a great alternative until you can afford something better.

Don't sleep on Book Brush. They're going to be a lot bigger than they are currently.

LOGISTICAL PROBLEMS WITH FORMATTING

I still haven't released the paperback version of my book *150 Self-Publishing Questions Answered.* I wrote it with The Alliance of Independent Authors (ALLi).

The book is supposed to have a neat feature that is a hybrid between a glossary and an index called a "glindex."

Originally, as ALLi and I were producing the book, we thought that it would be as simple as sending the Vellum file to the indexer to add the "glindex" into it. Boy, were we wrong.

Five months later, and we're still working through the best way to do it. Normally, I would have just published the paperback without the glindex, but this is an important element for ALLi to get right.

I learned far more about book typesetting than I ever thought I would. Book indexers have a certain way of speaking, and they're not always the easiest to follow.

I'm confident we'll get it done, but suffice to say that indexes are way more complicated than they seem. There's a reason why there are indexers who make a living doing this stuff.

Oh, things you learn when you've been doing this a long time...

BECOME A DATA-DRIVEN WRITER

GLOBAL LINK LOCALIZATION
UPDATE

In Volume 1 of this series, I discussed how I implemented a link localization service. In the author context, link localization is when a link directs readers to the proper Amazon store depending on their country. This is helpful because you don't have to worry about sending people to Amazon.com and them not being able to buy anything there because they live in another country. It's also helpful because you can improve your Amazon Associates income.

Anyway, I wanted to report on how that is going.

Since implementing link localization in the second quarter of 2020, I have received over 1,000 clicks on my localized links, which have redirected readers in 64 countries. Only 46% of that traffic was from the United States, which in my opinion is a solid number, as it shows my traffic is not overly dependent on the United States, which is a trap a lot of US authors fall into.

I watched my non-US Amazon affiliate income grow approximately 1200%. While the starting numbers were quite small, I'll take any increase I can get! I'm also starting to see Amazon Associates income from Australia, Canada, and

Europe—that's never happened for me in the eight years I've been publishing.

The investment has already paid for itself, and it hasn't even been a year yet. Probably one of the best ROI decisions I've made this year.

This is a win for the following reasons:

- I am doing the right thing for readers around the world and creating a better buying experience for them.
- I am increasing my international reach.
- I am increasing my affiliate income, which is small, but small streams add up to mighty rivers.

Anyway, I wanted to make sure I provided an update, as I consider it another level up.

MY DATA SPIDEY SENSE IS TINGLING...

In Volume 2 of this series, I talked about Natural Language Processing (NLP) and an idea to use it to catch corrections that my editor has made in the past, as a way for me to send her cleaner manuscripts. My goal is to stop as many repeat mistakes as possible in order to reduce my long-term editing costs. It also frees up my editor to focus on more important items in the book. Plus, it just respects her time.

Every author's process for editing is different, but in my opinion, here are all of the steps that an author could follow if they wanted to ensure their book was as error-free as possible:

1. Author self-edits to catch obvious errors.
2. Author uses built-in writing app spellchecker to catch errors.
3. Author uses Microsoft Word spell-checker (if it's not their primary writing app).
4. Author uses an advanced spelling and grammar checker like Grammarly or ProWritingAid.
5. Author uses beta readers to catch more errors.
6. Author uses a professional copyeditor.

7. Author uses a professional proofreader.
8. Author may use Word, ProWritingAid, or Grammarly (again).
9. Author may use a "typo squad" to help them catch errors after they publish the book, giving readers a way to report typos.

Here's my problem with the process: it's redundant even if you don't follow all of the steps, and it's not terribly effective. What about repeat mistakes that your editor catches? That's not contemplated in the steps. Therefore, you're doomed to follow the same process over and over again without any incremental improvements other than what you can *remember* to fix next time.

I can't remember what I ate for dinner last night, so there's no way I can remember what grammatical errors I made in my last book...

That's where this project comes in. Spell-checkers only get me so far. I want to create a system that "learns" my style and gets better with every book I write. And I want it to proactively catch errors that my editor would have caught.

I have been taking baby steps toward working on this project. This quarter, I took a few more.

The first step is to figure out some way to "capture" my editor's edits so that I can translate as many of them into if-then statements as possible. If you can turn something into an if-then statement, then you can (potentially) turn it into a command that a computer can understand, assuming the computer can understand the variables.

Granted, I can't do this with all the editor's edits, but if I could turn a handful of them into if-then statements that a Microsoft Word *macro* or an NLP engine can capture, it would make a gigantic difference in the internal consistency of my books.

In order to do this, I need to stop thinking about my manuscript as a series of words, but instead, a series of data points.

When I uncover opportunities like this, I can't stop thinking about them. I am relentlessly curious. I dig, dig, dig until I find a strand of yarn. Then I pull on that strand, and the whole problem unravels.

After much searching, I found a random website on the Internet around 3 AM one night. It advertised a free Microsoft Word add-in that allows you to extract data from your manuscript—most importantly, tracked changes. You can export all of your editor's tracked changes (and comments) to a table in a separate Word document.

This was the strand of yarn I was looking for—I just didn't realize it would be this easy.

Let me show you some images how it works. This is how the tracked changes table looks:

And here is how the acronym table looks:

Acronym	Definition	Page
ALL		40
COVID		11
EPUB		14
FOREVER		34
GDPR		17
NOT		45
RWA		7
SEO		1
TRUST		41
USDA		44
YOU		41
YOUR		36

Most people would yawn at this. Why is this even important? Because if you can create a table, then you can copy AND paste it into Microsoft Excel, where it is much more workable.

I pasted my edits table into Excel and added additional columns to help me tag and categorize the different types of edits.

Once in Excel, I added to the table, summarizing my lesson learned and where I thought it could be addressed by a Word macro or NLP:

And here's the last part of the table that contains some *rough* if-then statements:

If	Then
If a preposition is followed by noun phrase that includes a proper noun	Insert comment: Check for dropped article between the two nodes
If words "my current" exist	Insert comment: Verify "my." Editor flagged the words "my current" in past and replaced them with "the current"
Macro/if "notce/noticed that" exists … AI if VERB precedes "that	Insert comment: "Check "that". Include link to a "that" resource"
"Writers' conferences" exists	Replace with "writer's' conferences"
"bill of rights" or "Bill of rights" or "bill of Rights" exists	Replace with "Bill of Rights"
"Constitution" or "Constitutions" are capitalized	Lower case them with a comment: "Unless it is the United States Constitution, constitution should be lowercase."
If a comma precedes the word "too"	Delete the comma as a tracked change
Say/Says/Said/Ask/Asks/Asked/Shout/Shouts/Shouted/Yell/Yells/Yelled is not succeeded by a comma or a period	Insert comment: "Check dialogue construction. Introducing dialogue after a said-type phrase should always be done with a comma."

And some more if-then statements:

If	Then
If dialogue opens with a lowercase character and dialogue is NOT preceded by Say/Says/Said/Ask/Asks/Asked/Shout/Shouts/Shouted/Yell/Yells/Yelled + comma	Replace first letter of the dialogue with a capital letter
preposition is followed by a plural noun	Insert comment: Check for dropped article
If a less than two commas exists in a sentence: the sentence does not contain a simple list of items, and the word there is only one instance of the word "and"	Insert comment: Consider adding commas for clarity, particularly before in the final phrase
the word "but" is preceded by plural noun	Insert comment: Consider adding a comma before "but" for clarity.
The words "at first" are not followed by a comma, period, or semi-colon	Insert comment: Consider adding a comma after "at first" for clarity.

Please note that the rules on this table are specific to my writing only, not a declaration of how *you* should write your books. These are errors that my editor has caught that I agreed with. Some of them are purely stylistic.

Ultimately, I need to figure out:

1. How many errors I can program into Microsoft Word macros (which, in my opinion, can serve as another layer of grammar checking that Word's grammar checker can't do).
2. How many errors are leftover that can be programmed into an NLP engine.

3. How many errors are exclusively in my editor's realm.

So if you think about the editing process as a sieve:

1. The errors that spelling and grammar checkers can catch are big rocks that the sieve catches.
2. The errors that my editor catches are small rocks.
3. The errors my macros catch are fine particles that the sieve catches.
4. The errors my NLP engine catches are even finer particles that the sieve catches.
5. The errors that the writing apps, my editor and I miss are the grains of sand that flow through the sieve.

I want my editing sieve to catch as much as possible. The macro and NLP system adds an additional layer of protection.

In analyzing the first ten pages of one of my writing books, I found repeat mistakes of one of my biggest frustrations: dropped articles. I don't know an app that can catch them. The human eye frequently misses them because the brain pretends they're there. Even editors miss them all the time. Readers miss them too, but when they catch them...it's embarrassing.

In just two examples in the sample book I reviewed, the dropped article followed a preposition and came before a plural noun. For example: "Even her coworkers teased her about [the] novels she carried..."

Another time, the dropped article followed a preposition and came before a proper noun phrase:

"I worked at [a] Fortune 100 insurance company."

The rules of the English language dictate that prepositions and articles accompany each other frequently. If I want to catch a dropped article, I should start with the preposition and the following noun. They might offer clues for how to teach my system to predict situations for when an article might be dropped. I won't be able to catch them all, but by God, if I can catch a few...

This process also raises some philosophical questions about natural language processing: Can NLP identify rhetorical devices such as anaphoras? I'd love the ability for a program to spot common rhetorical devices such as anaphoras and help me identify if I'm not using them correctly. (Martin Luther King Jr.'s "I Have a Dream" speech is the most famous anaphora ever. He repeats "I have a dream" over and over—that's the anaphora.)

Also, can natural language processing detect proper noun phrases? Take "Fortune 100 insurance company." If you extract the proper noun from that sentence, Word only recognizes "Fortune." It doesn't understand "Fortune 100" unless you add it to the program's dictionary. And it doesn't understand the relationship between "Fortune 100" and "insurance company." Because of this, it can't detect subject-verb agreement, which explains why it missed the dropped article.

Yeah, this stuff is complicated. But it's fascinating.

Sure, I don't have time to code or create Word macros...I'm a writer after all. But I'm handy enough that I can create a prototype. Then I can pay someone to build what I need.

Word macros aren't difficult. You just have to understand how they work. I can easily do those myself after an hour or two of YouTube videos.

I don't know how much time and effort an NLP system would require. That's a big question mark that I'll learn as I continue on this journey. If it's too expensive, I can still pay someone to create a system based on my top ten or twenty offenders—that would still make a big difference. Either way, if I can figure this out, I don't see a scenario where I don't win in some way.

I've written so many books that I can probably find almost all of the programmable repeat mistakes by combing my existing work. After that, it's just adding a few new edits here and there with each new book.

Also, this system is retroactive. I can run my old manuscripts through it and catch previously missed errors, so that's an extra benefit too.

I believe that writers need to maximize the mileage out of the tools they have. Many are not, mainly because they don't know what their tools can do. No one (except me) wakes up in the morning and says, "I bet Microsoft Word macros can help me solve problems!" Nope. The very idea of Microsoft Word macros puts most writers to sleep. It's boring, too technical, and they can't see the benefit.

That's fine. While everyone else sleeps, I'll keep finding my strands of yarn...

AMAZON ADS HYPOTHESIS LOG

I've been focusing on Amazon Ads intensely this quarter. In fact, I have doubled my spending and created double the amount of my normal ads.

I do pretty well at Amazon Ads, so I can afford it. I haven't lost money as a whole on my ads since March. I want to see if I can double my income.

In my opinion, the hardest part about Amazon Ads is that it's hard to remember what you did or when you made a change.

I used to keep a journal of changes, but it didn't work because I didn't understand the ad data well.

Now I am much better at interpreting the ad data and I know what to do in almost every situation since I've been successful for almost a year now.

I need to get better about making hypotheses around the data and following up on them. You know, the responsible thing to do.

I started tracking my hypotheses, like "If I raise the budget for my automatic ads, then I should see more impressions within a week." Then, a week later, I check the hypothesis and go validate it.

This gives me a long-term look at the decisions I made.

It's a small but important step to help me make more data-driven decisions.

THE ADULTERATED DATA PROBLEM

Earlier this year, when I created my sales database, I arrived at a crossroads: did I want my database to contain *all* of my sales data or just the highlights?

The most important fields on any sales report are the date, title, marketplace or country, (net) units sold, and income. However, many retailers include unique fields that may be specific to the retailer, but not that useful to the author, such as book IDs. Kobo in particular includes a battery of cost of goods sold (COGS) and Value-Added Tax (VAT) fields that I honestly don't care about. Are these fields worth storing in the sales database?

I believe they are. In fact, I believe that you should store your reports as close as possible to the original format. You never know what you may need later.

Storing everything means you are storing what I call unadulterated data. You don't make any changes to it. The pros are that you keep everything in case you need it later and you also have some peace of mind. The con is that your database will be bigger over time and you're storing data you may never need.

You can choose to adulterate your sales data, which means that you only keep what you need and discard the rest. The pros are that you can focus on what's important and your database will be smaller. The con is that if you ever need the discarded data later, you won't have access to it. You'll have to refer to your raw sales reports to get the data you need, which is inconvenient.

Trackerbox, the popular (and only) sales tracking tool, operates under the adulterated data framework. It's one of the app's biggest drawbacks in my opinion.

Anyway, you may not find anything in this chapter useful in your career right now, but know that you'll need this knowledge someday.

DATA STEWARDSHIP

Most writers I know are terrified of Microsoft Excel. Whenever they open a spreadsheet, their foreheads get clammy, their hands sweat, their eyes glaze over, and fear paralyzes their brain from even doing the simplest arithmetic. I call it "spreadsheet-itis." Hundreds of thousands of writers suffer from it each year, but it's curable.

I used to be no different. I used to use spreadsheets in such a primitive manner that even the worst data analyst would have laughed me out of a room and blacklisted me from ever using Excel again.

I used to track all of my book royalties manually. I'd look at my various sales reports each month and I'd type in the amounts I made into a summary spreadsheet. It was so painful and agonizing that by the time I finished the data entry, I didn't want to *analyze* the data I spent so long entering. Plus, I made a ton of mistakes.

I invested in some Excel courses. It took a while, but I finally learned that I was doing everything backwards.

If you identified with anything I just wrote, then you have a *data entry* problem.

People hear the word data and tense up, but data is not scary. Data is objective and easy to understand. Getting to clean data is the difficult part, but only if you're uninitiated. And you can get yourself initiated by an hour or two's worth of videos on YouTube.

Data entry, on the other hand, is death. Few writers can tolerate it, and I suspect it's why most writers don't even bother tracking their sales.

Instead, we need to think of ourselves as data stewards. Instead of taking rows of data and manually moving them from Point A to Point B, we should instead let tools like Excel do the heavy lifting. Our job is to simply ensure the safe passage of the data.

When you think about data in this way, your approach changes. You start managing it at the highest levels instead of digging into minutia. And you can finally make decisions that will impact your writing business in a positive way.

The next time you're staring down a gruesome spreadsheet, or heaven forbid trying to get data from Point A to Point B, remember that you're a steward, and that avenues were designed to do the heavy lifting for you. If you invested your time and energy into discovering those avenues, how might your author business change for the better?

PRESTOZON

I discovered Prestozon, a service that helps you manage Amazon Ads using the power of artificial intelligence and machine learning. Prestozon helps you optimize your ads by giving you a better dashboard and deeper data analysis tools to make better decisions.

Prestozon intrigued me because I have said for the past year that I believe AI can run ads better than authors in the long-term. There are so many transactions per day across the entire industry of authors using ad platforms that an AI-assisted ad tool could optimize ads insanely well, and even aid with discoverability by finding links between books that authors wouldn't have thought of.

Well, the tool predated my idea, and it seems to be gaining attention and popularity. I haven't signed up for Prestozon because it uses a completely different methodology than I do to gauge the effectiveness of Amazon Ads. To use it would mean that I would have to change my entire approach, something I'm not ready to do yet.

I spent an evening watching their in-depth tutorial videos,

and I liked what I saw. If enough authors use the platform, it will get better.

If you need some help managing your Amazon Ads, check Prestozon out.

EMAIL WHILE WORKING FROM HOME DATA

I found an app that monitors my email inbox statistics. The service sent me a neat little report about how my email habits had changed since the beginning of the COVID-19 pandemic.

I sent 99% more emails during lockdown.

My response rate was identical compared to pre-COVID-19 times.

And I received 11% more emails.

Interesting data. Despite being in a lockdown, I still continued to respond to emails quickly despite receiving more emails overall.

Those emails aren't just "emails." They're questions from readers, amazing fan-mail, speaking opportunities, and so much more. But they're *relationships* first and foremost, and there is always a person on the other side of an email. It's cool to know that I'm continuing to keep my promises on my website around email service time.

THE POINT OF EXCEL

I don't consider myself to be an Excel expert, but my skills with the app are far better now than they were a year ago. I've invested a lot of time and energy into learning it. It also helped that I took a job late in the year where I spend five to six hours in Excel every day. That job was a blessing in disguise in my journey to become a data-driven writer...especially when you consider that my Excel skills before taking the job were the equivalent of a person who types with two fingers.

Anyway, that's why I am discussing Excel a lot in this volume. Learning it is an essential skill for any author who wants to become data-driven. I realized just how much I was missing when I finally understood how to use it. So many authors are terrified of spreadsheets, yet understanding how to use them correctly is one way to unlock opportunities in your writing life because you can see issues in your data. Act on those issues, and you'll make more money.

Many people think of Excel as a math tool, or a data analysis tool. Neither of those descriptions are true. Excel is a *logic* tool. You use the tools that Excel provides to apply logic to a problem so that you can solve it.

And in my experience, writers *excel* at logic (pun fully intended). We're masters of using logic to persuade and entertain people, but in the realm of spreadsheets, we don't know how to use that skill.

The more time I spend in Excel, the more I realize how little time I need to be spending there.

Excel masters don't spend hours in spreadsheets unless it's their job or they're building a tool. They open a spreadsheet, ask the right questions, get to the heart of the data, make a decision, and then get out. And they do it quickly. In minutes.

In fact, my goal with using Excel for my writing business is to make data-driven decisions in five minutes or less.

Why did my sales dip last month?

What's my best performing Amazon ad campaign, and what customer search terms are driving it?

What is my bestselling audiobook in the United Kingdom?

I need to be able to dive into Excel and answer these questions quickly. I'm nowhere near my goal of five minutes or less yet, but I can imagine how powerful my data skills will be when I get there!

That's a good goal for any writer to have. The less time you spend in a spreadsheet, the more you can write and market.

INTERFACING WITH THE
AMAZON API

An application programming interface (API) is a way for programmers to access data on a server without hacking or data scraping. In Amazon's case, they offer access to their backend data for developers to integrate the Amazon shopping experience directly into a website. There are many other ways to use the Amazon API.

I encountered a tool on YouTube that allows you to connect with the Amazon API directly from Microsoft Excel. You can enter an ASIN, and it will pull the data from Amazon into your spreadsheet. Very cool.

Some potential use cases:

- You could use this tool to pull in all the sales ranks for your book onto one spreadsheet so that you didn't have to check each book individually. Just refresh the spreadsheet.
- Amazon Advertising search term reports often give you ASINs for the books that your ads are being served on; in order to find the product information, you have to go to Amazon and search for the ASIN.

Imagine entering a bunch of ASINs in bulk, and in a few clicks getting the product information populated next to them in Excel.

- You could pull all the books in a category to get market intelligence, such as average price. There are better tools for this, though.

I won't share the app, as I'm ultimately not sure if this tool is a *sanctioned* use of the API. But I love the fact that it streamlines research and allows you to pull the data into the app you're already using.

I did not use the app because it requires an Amazon Seller account, which I do not have right now. But this is the future. Few people know that Excel can connect to APIs.

SPARKLINES

I discovered Microsoft Excel's Sparklines feature this quarter.

Sparklines are mini charts that fit within one cell but summarize data from another cell range.

Sparklines are useful on dashboards because they save space.

Most experienced Excel users know about Sparklines, but it was a neat discovery for me, especially as I think about creating a visual dashboard for my sales database.

CUSTOM DATA TYPES IN EXCEL

Excel offers a "data type" feature that, until now, has been limited. You could create cells with financial stock and geography data that updated in real-time. You could also add additional data without leaving Excel because *all* of the data attributes are contained in one cell.

If that sounds complicated, it's because it's not an easy concept to explain in writing. It makes more sense when you see it in action.

The Excel team released a new feature called "custom data types" that lets users create their own data sets to reference dynamically in a cell.

I've been waiting for this feature for a while. I have an idea to create custom data types for my books and their metadata.

Maybe I want to do a comparison in my sales database on how well books priced at $3.99 sell compared to $4.99. If I stored all of my book metadata as custom data, then I could overlay that on top of my sales database pivot.

I could also use the custom data set as the storage point for my book metadata rather than housing it in a separate database, making it easier and more portable.

URBAN FANTASY BOOK AND PARANORMAL ROMANCE BOOK DATABASE

In 2019, I created a tool called The Urban Fantasy and Paranormal Romance Book Database with my author friends John P. Logsdon and Ben Zackheim. The goal was to create a database of urban fantasy and paranormal romance that readers could search based on what they like to read.

Goodreads is a poor reading management tool. It does a lot of things right, but it's difficult to find anything on Goodreads beyond the subgenre level.

Yet, if you look at most urban fantasy books, the first thing that the book cover makes clear is what type of supernatural character the hero is.

What if you wanted to look for books where the hero was a werewolf?

What about a treasure hunter?

Good luck finding that on Goodreads. Listopia is where you would start, as that allows users to compile lists of books based on themes. But anyone can add books to a list, and the result is lists that aren't helpful.

Also, book discovery on Goodreads isn't useful. Despite the

website having an extremely complicated algorithm that was a pioneer ten years ago, it hasn't improved much since then.

That brings us back to urban fantasy. Goodreads isn't set up for how most urban fantasy and paranormal romance readers browse.

The Urban Fantasy and Paranormal Romance Book Database contains series in a giant database that you can filter and sort by:

- Series Name
- Author
- Protagonist Gender
- Protagonist Supernatural Type (Vampire, Werewolf, Necromancer, and so on)
- Protagonist Profession
- Setting
- Subgenre (of urban fantasy or paranormal romance)
- Publishing Type (traditional or self-published)
- Young Adult
- Paranormal Romance
- LGBTQ
- Reverse Harem
- Adult Language

So let's say for example that you wanted to find all of the non-paranormal romance wizard books by self-published authors. In a few clicks, you would have a list of series meeting those parameters, with links to the series on Amazon or the author's website.

Even better, anyone can add series to the database. If you're an urban fantasy or paranormal romance author, you can add your new series to it, so it's free marketing.

If you're a hardcore reader, you can bookmark it and use it for endless new reads.

Everyone wins.

As of this writing, here are some fun statistics:

- The database contains 315 series by 469 different authors
- The gender breakdown for protagonists is 68% female, 31% male, and 0.21% transgender.
- Most people would expect vampire heroes to dominate in the database; however, they only represent 7% of the books in the database.
- The top five most represented supernatural heroes are: witches, mages, faeries (fae), and most surprisingly, heroes with *no supernatural powers at all*.
- Seven percent feature LGBTQ protagonists.
- Students and cashiers were among the most represented professions.
- Sixty percent of the titles in the database were self-published.

I'll stop there. How cool is that data? I created the database so we could aggregate data about the urban fantasy genre. Sure, the database is still small, but readers are adding books to it regularly, and maybe one day it can encompass several thousand books and become *the* definitive resource for authors and readers in the genre.

The database has been helpful in my marketing efforts since my main genre moving forward will be urban fantasy.

BECOME THE WRITER OF THE FUTURE

2021 STRATEGY

Every October, I design my strategy for the coming year. I do it in October so that I'm done before the holidays. November and December pass at light-speed, and I don't like planning for the year in January after it has already started.

This year, I decided to share my author strategy publicly. I did this so that other people can see it and use it to think about their strategy.

The author community as a whole doesn't always do a good job of thinking long-term, so I'd like to try to influence that.

My mission as an author is to entertain and/or educate the niches that I serve, and to remain nimble.

Nimbleness is important. In a rapidly-changing publishing landscape where the future of traditional publishing is uncertain, indie authors' ability to pivot is an underrated asset. It's how we win, *and* how we stay relevant for decades to come.

Any good mission must be supported with strategic pillars.

You already know the five pillars of my author business because they comprise the structure of this book:

1. Become a world-class content creator

2. Become a world-class marketer
3. Become a technology-driven writer
4. Become a data-driven writer
5. Become the writer of the future

If I had to distill each strategic pillar into an essence, they would be:

1. Become a world-class content creator by developing a diverse and deep portfolio of work of the highest possible quality.
2. Become a world-class marketer by mastering the current tools on the market to improve my profit while simultaneously reducing my expenses and tax liability.
3. Become a technology-driven writer by creating technology-assisted writing business that helps me create world-class content and sell more products.
4. Become a data-driven writer by becoming a master of analyzing my author business data to unlock new opportunities hidden in plain sight.
5. Become the writer of the future by staying up-to-date with the industry, looking to the future, protecting the business, and making smart investments that will pay off in five to ten years.

Those are the high-level details. My strategy itself is far more tactical and analytical, so check it out if you're interested.

For me, 2021 will be the year when things finally converge: the years I spent learning and improving my craft, the investments in profitable advertising, mastering technology and using it in unique ways to streamline and automate my business, learning data analysis, studying the future, and most importantly, running a profitable author business.

Will I become a mega bestseller? No.

But many of the things I've invested in the last few years are starting to bear fruit, and I believe that I'll be able to start harvesting some of that fruit as early as 2021.

If you'd like to learn in greater detail how I will be carrying out my strategy, be sure to check out the interactive mindmap at www.authorlevelup.com/2021strategy.

I also recorded an hour-long livestream about my strategy in greater detail. Watch it at www.authorlevelup.com/2021strategyvideo.

DEVELOPING A READER FIRST
MENTALITY

This quarter, I published a book called The Reader's Bill of Rights: A Manifesto on How to Treat Your Readers Right.

In one of the chapters, I talk about fan-mail.

When you become a bestselling writer, you receive a ton of emails. I bet someone like George R.R. Martin receives hundreds if not thousands of emails every day. There's no way you can keep up with that amount.

But what if you could? What if someone at George R.R. Martin's level committed to providing a response to every reader that emailed them or sent them fan-mail?

Authors at that level have the least amount of time, but they're in the best position to address this problem. For example, there are systems that can read an email for sentiment analysis using artificial intelligence. That could divide the emails into "positive" and "negative," much like reviews on Amazon.

A certain percentage of the negative emails don't deserve a response—maybe they're laced with profanity, contain death threats, or something else that loses the sender the privilege of a dignified response. These emails can be handled by an assistant who can verify whether the sorting is correct. If so, with one click, the assistant can send these people a generic, standardized response. The author doesn't need to see these emails, and assistants who handle them should have access to mental health resources if needed.

For the negative emails that are constructive and productive, the assistant could scan them for certain keywords to determine which ones are the most important. The assistant could handle the majority of them, with the rest going to the author. The key criteria, in my opinion, would be whether the email will hurt the author's production or emotional mindset, or whether the email is part of a bigger trend that the author should know about. If the answer is yes, then the assistant handles the email and reports any trend findings to the author. Any leftover emails go into the author's queue.

For the positive emails, those can be segmented too. Some positive emails don't need a personal response. They might be a "just wanted to say thank you and keep up the good work" type email, or a "just an FYI, but..." Those can be addressed with a different standardized form letter, maybe with a coupon or a bonus short story or something.

There might also be positive emails that are best handled by an assistant, such as "what book should I read first?" or "when will the website be updated?"

All other positive emails are squarely in the author's realm. If someone sends an email about how the author's book changes their life, they deserve a response from the author, not the assistant. In my opinion, it doesn't matter how long it takes, as long as the author sets expectations properly on the contact form page of the website. Whatever the author promises is what the author should deliver. I bet that readers wouldn't even mind an absurd timeline like one or two years.

Imagine what readers would say if a mega bestselling author did this, and if they received a thoughtful response to their fan mail. First, their heads would explode. Second, they'd buy *more* of that author's books. Third, they'd tell their friends.

What an amazing opportunity for a big-name author to make long-lasting impacts on their fans, and even more money in the process.

Would it be possible to respond to every email? Of course not. Fans know that. But if someone sends you a thoughtful email praising you and telling you about the impact your work has had on them, that's a super fan. Most readers don't do that. Super fans deserve the best because they'll stick with an author for a long, long time.

Any investment in assistants or software would pay for itself.

But, as I say frequently, I'm an alien. I don't think like most people. Most people look for ways to minimize their contact with fans as they become more successful. A classic example of this is creating a forum or Facebook group and then only popping in once or twice a year.

But I believe that your link with your fans is vital. The more you stay in contact with them, the more information they'll give you about how to keep them happy. And if you do it right, you can do this without ever compromising your art.

THE EMPLOYEES OF THE WRITER
OF THE FUTURE

In a moment of weakness, I was watching some YouTube videos of Kim Kardashian.

It's amazing how many people follow her around on a daily basis. Assistants, makeup artists, and so on.

It got me thinking about a silly idea: if I was a filthy rich multi-millionaire author on the level of Stephen King or Nora Roberts, what would my staff look like? I doubt I'd have people following me around, except if I traveled to writing events, but I would definitely have a team, as I couldn't do it alone.

And yes, this chapter will be vain, but don't pretend that you haven't had these daydreams!

Let's assume that I continued the same activities I am doing today. Writing like crazy, YouTubing, podcasting, public speaking, and so on. I'd be doing them on a bigger scale.

First, I would need a chief of staff or operations manager. Entrepreneur and virtual assistant expert Chris Ducker calls this a "general virtual assistant"—someone who manages the details of the day-to-day operations. For example, they would manage my other assistants, manage my calendar, control the flow of certain information to me such as fan-mail trends, control *access* to me, handle some of my personal affairs, and so on. My chief of staff would need to be someone I can trust, probably someone who has the opposite personality type of me. They need to be a whip-cracker, and, to use the famous legal expression, have an iron fist in a velvet glove. (Trust me that I can exhibit those qualities too, but I'll be spending my time doing other things, remember.)

Next, I would have a dedicated customer service assistant. This person's job would be to keep my readers happy and delight them in other small and unexpected ways. A professional, cheerful attitude with a sales mentality is required. I have extremely high standards. This person would monitor my email inbox and triage it accordingly (see my chapter on fan-mail earlier in this book). They would handle refunds, ensure that readers who purchase products directly from me have a delightful experience, handling small problems before they become big ones. All roads would lead to my customer service person first, which is what makes this such an important position. They would be my secret weapon.

Next, I would need an audiovisual team—someone to edit my videos and someone to edit my podcasts. If I traveled to a speaking event, preferably my video editor would travel with me and film my speech and my interactions with readers, and maybe even content I might conduct for my YouTube channel on location. This person's sole job would be to make sure that I always look good and to capture as much content that we can repurpose later on the website, blog, YouTube channel, and more.

I would also need a marketing assistant. This person would, *under my direct supervision*, manage ad campaigns, handle social media posts, design promotional materials, and find ways to market my existing catalogue. This person would *never* have access to any of my financial information. That's very, very important. So many authors are happy to give away access to their bank account or wave their hands and let their assistant handle their financial affairs. Nope. Not with me.

And lastly, I would contract with a few individuals who wouldn't be full-time employees, but they would provide regular services:

- An editor, proofreader, and cover designer who would prioritize my work. My chief of staff would coordinate them and prepare my books for publication according to my standards, with me having the final say.
- An intellectual property attorney on retainer to handle lawsuits (since mega bestsellers get sued all the time). The attorney would also advise me on urgent legal matters as they come up, like Hollywood contracts, for example. The attorney would also handle occasional copyright infringement situations where someone is infringing on my IP and I need to stop it.
- An accountant.
- A financial advisor and a tax attorney, as I would be making purchases and investments in the name of the business for tax purposes.
- A bodyguard, if necessary.
- An IT security expert on retainer who would help me secure my network and the computers of employees working for me. As a mega bestseller, I would be a target for cyber attacks and ransomware attacks. The expert would help me minimize vulnerabilities and ensure that my work and products are always available, always protected, and that I can restore them if needed. They would also

ensure that my employees don't inadvertently expose my networks. Not an easy job.

Subtract the salaries of all these wonderful folks from my annual salary and I'd still have money to burn!

As for me and my daily activities, I would need all these people because my days would be spent:

- Sharpening my overall author strategy and vision
- Writing like a madman
- Engaging with my fans
- Traveling and making public appearances
- Finding new revenue streams
- Negotiating licensing agreements
- Managing the financials of the business
- Developing relationships with fellow authors and key players in the industry
- Managing my staff

What a daydream! Maybe some day it will happen.

WHAT'S YOUR MAGIC NUMBER?

I'm nowhere near making a full-time living for my work, but I thought about what it would take for me to go full-time in a perfect world. How much money would I need to make? In other words, what's the "magic number?"

I thought about this one day. I added up:

- my average monthly business expenses with a padding of ten percent to account for growth, since my expenses increase from time to time.
- my average household expenses with a padding of ten percent.
- my average "contingency" expenses (leaking toilets, car trouble, home improvements, and so on).

The sum of those three items is my magic number, but it's not that easy.

How much money would I need in my business and personal savings accounts as a cushion? I'd need at least eighteen month's worth of expenses, and honestly, that's not enough.

The writing life is cyclical. Sometimes you have high

months and then you have low months. How do I factor that into the equation?

And what about how I want the business to *look* when I go full-time? Ideally, many of the projects and investments I'm making right now would streamline, automate, and outsource many tasks that I'm doing manually today. My hope would be that the business would be as optimized as I can make it, possibly with an assistant in place helping me run some of the day-to-day operations. Me stepping into a full-time role is the last piece of the puzzle, an accelerant that will help grow sales even more.

Of course, life is never perfect. It's not that easy. Few people get to command their destinies on their own terms. A lot of people are forced to go full-time before they're ready because life happens. That could very well be my situation too. But I believe it pays dividends to *think* about your future because it can inform your decision-making.

TRACKABLE EXPENSES AND ROI

Every writer has expenses. They're vital to running an author business.

But a question I've been asking lately is "how is my spending supporting my strategy, and how can I spend in a way that drives revenue?"

While logging my expenses, I've started to assign return on investments to them. This isn't possible with everything, but I wanted to know how many of my expenses for the year directly resulted in revenue that was more than the expense itself. Then, in theory, I could subtract those expenses from my overall expense amount, which would give me an adjusted expense amount that more accurately reflected what my "true" expenses were for the year. It would also potentially clue me in to how much I'm "wasting" each year—i.e. an expense that I cannot directly tie to revenue.

A few examples:

- I hired my video editor to edit my video for a virtual speaking event this quarter. The amount of books during the event offset the amount I paid him so that I made a small profit from the event. Many of the comments viewers made during the event were around my video production, so I can assume that the gamble paid off and netted more sales than if I hadn't hired him. Thus, I can subtract a week's worth of video editing expenses from my overall expense amount.

- I hired an illustrator to create maps for my book *The Indie Author Atlas*. After I signed off on the work, I found a typo that I accidentally missed. I would have had to hire her again, which would have cost approximately $25. Earlier this year, I purchased an app called Affinity Publisher, which surprisingly, allowed me to edit the source file of the map in question. Affinity cost me $25. I originally thought that Affinity would have been a "dud" purchase because my needs changed after I bought it, but it paid for itself.

Those are two examples. They're minor, but my hypothesis was that if I did this exercise on all of my expenses for the year, I bet I could find savings. And I did.

This type of thought exercise works best with operational expenses. It's not as helpful when looking at your production or marketing expenses, because that requires different, longer term thinking. Some of your books might not turn a profit for a few years, if ever. But what about an app that you purchase a one-time license for?

Some other ways to think about this:

- How can equipment and applications you buy for your writing business pay for themselves?

- Do the subscriptions you pay for on an annual basis pay for themselves? If they don't, what other justification can you make? Maybe they save you time or improve your reader experience. That's valid too. If you can't find a justification, can you cut the expense?
- What percentage of your expenses can you quantify with hard dollars? Knowing that you can't do this for everything, is there a "right" number?

To make this more concrete, let's use a common author example.

Most authors purchase a subscription to an email marketing service. Let's say you pay $100 per year. How would you tie revenue to this expense? Easy. When you launch a book and send an email to your fans, look at how much you make within 48 hours after you send the email. Over the course of the year, is that number more or less than $100? If you're a new author, it'll probably be less—so don't cut it. Just understand the number, as it would be unwise to stop email marketing just because you have a small audience. But if you're a more experienced author, it's smart to know how much revenue your email platform drives for you each year. It also helps you justify upgrades. For example, I had to upgrade my email service this year, which cost me around $75 extra per year. Since I know how much money my emails drive each year on average, I knew I could afford it.

Let's show how this can make a big difference in how you view your expenses each year. Assume that you spend $5,000 this year for writing expenses. Your budget is $4,500, which means you overspent by $500. Not good, right?

What if you were able to show that $250 of your expenses paid for themselves and/or drove more money than you spent?

First, subtract the $250 from your total expenses. You now have a $250 overage.

So if you look at your total amount for the year, you would have exceeded your budget by 11% ($5,000 divided by $4,500).

But if you use the adjusted amount instead, you only exceed your budget by 5% ($4,750 divided by $4,500). So you're still over for the year, but by a little less.

What if your average adjusted expenses resulted in a 5% difference each year? What if the next year you were more cost conscious, coming in at around $4,600 in total expenses? You'd go from a 2% overage to a 97% underage.

What if you had a year where you came in under budget already? Well, then a 5% difference would show an even *better* performance.

It's great if you "stumble" into this number, but what would happen if you became more intentional about it? What if you could improve this number?

It's an interesting thought exercise because it forces you to quantify your expenses with hard dollars, which can at times be painful, especially in the beginning of your career when you don't know what you should be buying.

If you did this exercise, what would the difference between *your* total expenses and *your* "true" expenses be?

I like this exercise because it stacks up with other "invisible" numbers in your writing business.

For me, business is revenue minus expenses, which equals profit.

Increase your revenue by diversifying your revenue streams, improving your marketing, and expanding your portfolio.

Spend strategically in a way that increases your revenue and helps your expenses pay for themselves as much as possible.

Find areas in your writing business where technology and data can help you streamline, automate, and outsource your daily tasks, which reduces your expenses further (and possibly increases your revenue).

Reduce your tax liability to increase the amount of profit you keep every year.

All of these tactics work together to help you maximize the impact of your art and run a sustainable business.

DEALING WITH CRITICISM

Gary Vaynerchuk did a great video on criticism on his YouTube channel. A young woman was telling him about her struggles with self-doubt. She struggled because other women told her that she was inadequate and not capable enough to follow her dream. She had developed a sizable Instagram following but never felt like she was good enough to have the success that she built.

Gary told her that she needs to think about her body like armor. That armor blocks bad criticism, but it also blocks the really good criticism too. He mentioned how someone replying with a comment like "you're the best" is a quick sugar high. We crave those comments, and because we allow ourselves to be open to *those*, that also lets in the really bad comments. The solution he offered was to take less stock in the really positive comments. Read them, appreciate them, and move on. Don't fall for the sugar high. By doing that, the really negative comments would affect her less.

I found it to be sound advice, and definitely true for me. I'm just passing it along.

PROCRASTINATION AS STRESS RELIEF

I subscribe to Mel Robbins's YouTube channel. I like her worldview and her positivity. I also think her type of vulnerability is most similar to mine.

Mel answered a question in one of her videos about how to deal with procrastination. She called procrastination a form of stress relief.

I used to call procrastination a lot of things. Stress relief wasn't one of them. But it makes sense when you think about it.

We procrastinate because putting off the task we need to do feels good in the short term, even though it's painful in the long-term. In some cases, procrastination can be helpful, particularly if we need to come up with a creative solution to an idea. But for reasons we all know, it can also be harmful.

I have had many times this year where I've put things off, even though I knew I needed to do them. For example, at the time I'm writing this chapter, I should have finished this book and sent it to my editor by now. But I kept putting it off because I chased other things that were more important to me at the time.

I'm not advocating for people to procrastinate to feel better. But understanding the emotion is key to learning how to defeat it.

TALENT + ENDURABILITY = SUCCESS

I was listening to a podcast and the guest (a very successful career writer in the literary genre) said something interesting.

She said that there are a lot of writers in the world with talent. Sometimes they waste their talent. Sometimes they don't realize they have talent and self-destruct, or do things that squander their gift. Sometimes they make bad life decisions. Or they're just impatient, or they can't handle rejection and uncertainty.

She gave a simple equation. Talent + endurability = success.

Not everyone has talent, but you can work on it. As Dean Wesley Smith says, talent is just a measure of a writer's skill at a point in time.

Anyway, the writer continued with an explanation of endurability. Endurability is more than resilience. It's the ability to keep going even though others tell you that your work isn't good; it's the ability to keep walking in the dark and leading without followers.

I'm paraphrasing her, but I believe the quote below is mostly right (I typed it as I was listening, so forgive me): endurability is about good habits, patience, discipline, ability to shrug off rejection, the ability to not be self-destructive, the ability to not get in one's own way, to make good lifestyle choices, to not become a drug addict or an alcoholic...to persist and to honor one's gift, and to understand that to have a gift is a precious thing, and to nurture it, give it the time and space that it needs, and not give in to the demands of the rest of the world, which does not exist to nurture your gift."

Wow. I'll just leave that there for you to digest.

WRITERS AS WHALES

When I finished my Beast Mode challenge, I started my Amnesia Mode challenge. Re-learning marketing after such a prolific period of writing felt weird, like I was out of my element.

It reminded me of a whale.

When I'm writing, I'm in the water. I'm feeding on plankton, exploring the world, and communicating with other "writer whales." It's where I love to be.

But I can't breathe underwater. I have to come up to the surface for air. Air gives me life. And that air is marketing. Without it, I can spend as much time in the water as I want, but my explorations and feeding sessions won't bear any fruit.

Yet, if I spend too much time out of the water, I'll die. So it's a delicate balance.

What's your balance? For me, I tend to spend too much time in the water and I don't come up for air nearly as much as I should. If I don't change that, it'll be hard to become a true writer of the future. Some writers are too scared to go into the water and stay near the surface. They're marketing geniuses, but their craft is shallow.

How might thinking of yourself as a whale change your perspective in how you approach writing craft and marketing?

ACX RETURNS CONTROVERSY

ACX caused controversy this year when they announced that Audible customers could refund or exchange an audiobook up to a year after purchase. The refund would come from the author's royalties.

The backlash was swift, and many author organizations sprang into action, including The Alliance of Independent Authors (ALLi), who were instrumental in mobilizing people against the measure.

Audible relented quickly and offered some concessions, but the issue is still ongoing at the time of this writing.

I'm proud of ALLi for their efforts in this area, and that's exactly why I pay them yearly dues. (If you're not a member, join using my paid link at www.authorlevelup.com/Alli).

PAYMENT SPLITTING: A NEW TREND TO WATCH

I was delighted to see Draft2Digital offer a payment-splitting option this quarter. I wrote about PublishDrive's Abacus in the previous volume of this series, which offers a similar function.

The nice part about Draft2Digital's service is that it *actually* splits the payments, whereas Abacus simply tells you what is due to your collaborator. Also, there's no cost, which makes this far more compelling than Abacus, which requires an annual fee. There's also no hassle, as your split payments are automatically reflected in both your and your co-author's monthly sales reports.

That's the proper way to do it.

Oooh, healthy competition! How often do you see that in the self-publishing space?

Payment splitting is now officially a trend. It's hard not to imagine every major distributor offering this feature now. It's also a market opportunity for any new retailers in the future— "Publish with us and we'll split your royalties with co-authors at no cost."

Ultimately, payment splitting is an important trend to

watch because it minimizes risk. Instead of worrying about whether your co-author is stealing from you, you can simply look at the accounting that both of you agreed to. It also makes it easier to create box sets and other collaborative works.

DIRECT AUDIOBOOK SALES

Book Funnel expanded its services this year, branching into delivering audiobooks as well as ebooks.

Audiobooks are difficult to deliver. They often contain chapters that are very large MP3 files, and you can't host them on your website without getting in trouble with your hosting provider.

It makes sense that Book Funnel would want to help with the hosting. Now you can sell audiobooks directly on your website through a service like Payhip or Gumroad and let Book Funnel handle the fulfillment.

I implemented direct ebook sales onto my *Author Level Up* site early in the quarter, but I didn't incorporate direct audiobook sales, even though I could have. There are still too many problems, namely the listening experience.

Book Funnel will deliver the book as a series of MP3s to the customer, who then has to load them into their music player and sync the music to their mobile device, which is not terribly difficult. But your average reader may not know how to do that. They also lose the ability to listen to audiobooks with:

- speed tracking
- 15- or 30-second skip-aheads and replays
- the ability to jump around the audiobook easily
- sleep timers

These are common features on audiobook and podcast apps, and readers are accustomed to them. They may not have an appetite for listening to an audiobook on, say, Apple's Music app.

There is another service called Authors Direct that allows you to sell audiobooks directly to your readers, and they can download and listen via a dedicated app that functions similar to most major audiobook apps. In my opinion, this is a more reader-centric option, more preferable for me. I still applaud Book Funnel for offering an alternative, as there will be readers who are fine with just receiving the MP3s and don't want to fuss with *another* app on their phone. It's much like readers who prefer PDFs—they usually don't need any help getting the book onto their device of choice.

The ideal solution would be to give the reader a choice at the point of sale how they want to consume the audio. Some may want a dedicated app, and others may just want the MP3s. Depending on what they choose, the author can flex accordingly —send them a Book Funnel link or send them a code so they can download the book onto the Authors Direct app.

This gets more complicated when you consider AI-narrated audio. That would likely need a dedicated app. Can Authors Direct handle such technology? Probably not yet, but that's asking a lot at this early point in the technology's life.

So, as I think about direct audio sales, I think about:

- The buying experience and how easy it is to make a purchase.

- The ability to add coupon codes.
- The ability to upsell and cross-sell.
- The logistics of getting the audio from point of sale to the reader's preferred method of listening, which is still a difficult challenge right now.
- Future capabilities. If I want to sell AI-narrated audio *and* human-narrated audio directly to readers, will I have to use separate services? Or will this service manifest itself in ways we're not thinking of yet, such as Audible offering the service as a value-add to its existing app, with no real alternatives for doing this direct for a few years until others catch up?

I will probably pursue Authors Direct in the near future, but long-term, I'd like the ability to sell *everything* direct under a unified storefront. If you want to sell direct today, you have to use *at least* three different storefronts on your website:

- An ebook storefront such as Gumroad or Payhip.
- A paperback storefront such as Ae.rio or Bookshop.
- An audio storefront such as Authors Direct.

Very, very clunky right now. It's hard to be a world-class content creator and marketer when you offer such vastly different buying experiences. It's also harder to service your customers.

This is a developing area that I'm tracking closely, because it will get better.

IDEAS YOU CAN STEAL

PART-TIME EMAIL ONLY ASSISTANT

I'm almost at the point where I need to hire an assistant to help with my email. Ironically, I am *not* in a position to need an assistant in other areas of my business because the work load isn't high enough yet.

I priced an assistant who can provide a la carte email service. I can pay them for an hour or two to clean out my inbox when it overflows.

I've been able to achieve inbox zero and stay there for about a month at the time of this writing. I find that if I can get to inbox zero, I can stay there for a long time. But the moment my emails rise past one hundred, I'm buried. All it takes is a vacation, busy season at work, or law school exams—and in less than a week, my inbox is a disaster.

I'm considering hiring a virtual assistant as needed when:

- I'm on vacation for longer than one week with no laptop access. The emails that cause me the most trouble are the ones I can't reply to right away because I need to be at my laptop to answer it.

- During the two weeks leading up law school exams and the week after.
- When I'm overwhelmed and need help.

Sure, it's an expense, but it's worth paying to dig myself out of that hole. The last time my emails rose over one hundred, the following things happened:

- Reader fan-mail went unanswered for almost a week, which is unusual for me.
- I missed sales opportunities.
- I overlooked important emails, making me look unprofessional.

Paying an assistant for a couple hours of work to achieve peace of mind is worth it.

THE INDIE AUTHOR BOUNTY HUNTER

No, I'm not advocating for hunting authors and taking them to jail. "The Indie Author Bounty Hunter" is the catchiest title I could come up with for what is really a "quality assurance professional."

When you have as many books as I do, it's difficult to keep track of everything. Imagine if I could pay a "bounty hunter" to review the following for typos or errors:

- my website(s)
- my social media profiles
- my books' sales pages
- my books' samples
- my books' interiors

I'd pay them a flat fee and then a "bounty" for every error they find. They would return a list of errors along with an invoice. Then, I could fix the problems and rest assured that my platform is as error-free as possible.

Of course, you could also pay an assistant to do this work,

but it would be expensive. A bounty hunter could do it faster since it's the only thing they do.

This could be a great way for someone with superior attention to detail to make some money on the side. It's also an idea that an existing author-centric virtual assistant could incorporate into their service offerings.

WRITING WHILE MOVING

I recently bought a recumbent exercise bike so I could get healthier. The bike includes a desk attachment so I can put a laptop or a book on it while I exercise. I've used the bike while calling into webinars and meetings that don't require me to participate.

One day while pedaling, I had an interesting idea—what if I wrote a book *only* while moving? What if, every time I got on the exercise bike, I wrote a book (or dictated one)? What if exercise time was the only time I could work on the book? How many words would I write each session, and how long would it take me to write the book?

What would my book look like in terms of "miles," "calories," and "pounds lost?" What would one book represent in each of those categories?

Posture issues and health concerns aside, it's such a cool idea if I could do it safely. It would also be great content for my YouTube channel.

Don't be surprised if you see a chapter in a future volume about "writing while moving." The idea won't let me go.

AUTHOR IT COOPERATIVE

Every author has a need to hire an IT professional at some point in their career. Websites crash. WordPress doesn't cooperate. You want a new feature on the site. All of that requires money, and website programmers aren't cheap.

The idea is for authors to pool their resources for IT support. The group would contract with a dedicated programmer who would perform monthly routine services on the authors' website, and they'd troubleshoot any issues that come up. They'd also offer one-off services at a discounted rate per author.

This could be an affordable way to pay for IT services that would ordinarily price smaller authors out of access.

21-DAY CHALLENGE

I encountered a "21-Day Diversity and Equity Challenge" on the Internet. The goal was for a person to become more sensitive to issues around diversity and inclusion in 21 days through a series of online exercises, webinars, and videos.

While I don't know how effective an idea like this is in combating the diversity and inclusion problem, I liked the idea itself.

What's the most important thing you need to learn as an author right now, and can you design a 21-day challenge around it?

If you're a nonfiction author or content creator, what's the most important idea that your audience faces right now, and can you develop a 21-day challenge and invite them to join you as you help them solve the problem? Even better, can you time it around the new year?

That's why I like the idea. It takes 21 days to develop a habit, so a challenge like this can make a real difference in your life.

YEAR OF CHALLENGES

In the last chapter, I discussed 21-day challenges. What if you spent an entire year doing 21-day challenges?

That would be around 17 challenges!

What if each challenge leveled up your writing game just a little? What if you did each challenge publicly? How would you grow?

If I were new to the industry, knowing what I know now, here would be some of my 21-day challenges:

1. Read 3 bestselling books in my subgenre similar to my book
2. Scrivener mastery challenge (or substitute your favorite writing app)
3. Time management challenge
4. Half-novel challenge (1500 words per day)
5. Short story challenge (21 short stories in 21 days)
6. Back-in-time challenge (pick your favorite writing podcast and listen to one backlist episode you've never heard per day)

7. Study the masters challenge part 1 (pick your favorite contemporary author and spend 21 days learning from their interviews and content about writing, like a mentorship)

8. Study the masters challenge part 2 (for that same contemporary author, study one of their books and find one new writing craft technique to use per day)

9. Book formatting challenge (learn one new thing about book formatting each day)

10. Website creation challenge (learn one new thing about websites so you can build yours afterward)

11. Email marketing challenge (learn one new thing about email marketing per day)

HISTORY OF A CERTAIN SUBGENRE

The literary world is full of genres and subgenres, and each one has its own unique history. You can probably find a book that has the "history of romance novels" for example, but what about the history of romantic suspense? Who were the pioneering authors in the genre? How did they market their work? What did readers think about the first books? What did the covers look like? What does the genre look like today?

In my opinion, that's fascinating fodder for a book, podcast, or YouTube channel. You become a "historian" of a genre and piece together a history of a subgenre through thorough research, interviews, and travel to conferences. If done correctly, it would provide incredible context for authors writing in the genre who don't know the history of it. A lot of that history is dying with older authors.

In my case, I'd love to read a history of the urban fantasy genre—one that includes the contributions paranormal romance authors *and* self-published writers. I'd also love to follow someone who has their finger on *all* aspects of the genre: readers, writers, and publishers, industry sales, emerging trends, and so on.

Like many of my ideas, this one would require someone with the right personality.

AI FOR SLUSH PILES

I was reading an installment of Jane Friedman's *The Hot Sheet*, which is a bi-weekly periodical of the newest developments in the publishing industry.

In one article, she wrote about the emergence of spelling and grammar apps that are specific to the publishing industry, unlike Grammarly, which is for general audiences. One service was called Fixional, which looks and functions similarly to Grammarly. However, it is designed for editors. Here's what Friedman wrote: "Speaking at Digital Book World, the cofounder and CEO, Pierce Gaynor, explained that Fixional can be taught what kind of writing your publication wants to acquire and publish. For example, the company currently works with a publisher that receives about 1,000 manuscripts per month and has 10,000 manuscripts awaiting review—but only five editors to go through it. (Anyone who works at a literary journal will know the feeling.) Fixional was fed all the work the publisher had already accepted and published, then allowed editors to filter and sort the slush pile based on various criteria from the published work, such as quality, completeness, and clarity. Editors can now scale their judgment and expertise over thousands of manuscripts at a time."

Interesting. So editors can teach the app what types of works they want to read, and the AI filters the works accordingly. If you thought submitting to magazines was hard already...

I see upsides, though. First, if editors rely on the AI instead of, say, a submission assistant, that could mean that they could issue rejections faster, which would be a good thing for authors.

The second upside is what I believe will be the rise of database matching services for literary magazine submissions. A developer could, in theory, create an AI service that authors can submit their work to, and the service would examine the author's work, compare it to open magazine submissions (which use AI too), and then submit to magazines it believes is a good fit. All of this would happen without the author being involved. The author would pay a yearly fee. This could effectively end the submission process as we know it, replacing it with semi-automation. This technology may already exist in some form today.

A downside is cost. This type of software will be expensive for magazines to implement. An equivalent tool would also be expensive for authors. My biggest fear with artificial intelligence is the creation of a have and have-not society. Successful people and businesses will have access to AI and less successful people will not.

SHOWING THE ENTIRE PUBLISHING PROCESS LIVE IN ONE GIANT VIDEO

I've always thought it would be interesting to take the art of writing a book and turn it into a mini reality show. Every time you start working, turn the camera on. Sure, it would be weird, but people would find it endlessly fascinating, especially if you shared your screen. Bonus points if you livestream it.

Start from the beginning and let people watch as you conceive, outline, write, edit, format, work with a designer and editor, and publish a novel.

Put everything into one giant video on YouTube, add some production value, and monetize the hell out of it, with an ad every hour.

I have no idea what would happen, but it would be interesting. Fellow author Garrett Robinson did this a few years ago with his *Nightblade* series. He mostly does Twitch livestreams now.

I believe this idea would work because people are oddly intrigued by seeing "over artists' shoulders." It would also help them see new ways of working.

INCLUDING FAILURES ON YOUR ABOUT PAGE

On a podcast interview, someone talked about including failures on their resume. As a society, we place a premium on people's successes, but we never see the string of failures that led them to success.

What if you include failures on your about page?

Here's what my about page would say:

- Published 50 books and counting and is still not a full-time author.
- Invested $30,000 in a writing business that failed to turn a profit for six years. And he still kept pouring money into it, even with minimal sales and all seemed lost.
- Signed at least six terrible copyright licensing agreements that he's still paying the price for.
- Produced three translated books that make zero dollars per month.
- Started three different podcasts and failed before he found success in the medium.
- Neglected marketing for six years.

- Spent over 15,000 hours devoted to the writing life with only slightly average results.

There are many more.

Seeing people's failures makes it easier to understand what they went through to get to where they are, and how much they had to sacrifice.

THE RETURN OF PERMAFREE?

When I started publishing in 2014, setting a book permanently free ("permafree") was a viable marketing option. The Amazon algorithms treated free books favorably and readers were kinder to free books than they are now (though not by much). However, Amazon changed its algorithms to decrease the visibility of free books, so many authors abandoned the strategy.

My book *Android Paradox* was permafree for about a year. It funneled a lot of new readers into my platform.

I've been hearing people say lately that permafree is still a viable strategy, especially if you are not exclusive to Amazon.

I'm considering trying it again with one of my series in conjunction with Amazon and/or Facebook advertising, just to see what happens. It may work, or it may not, but either way, it would be interesting to see what happens.

TAXES FOR AUTHORS

This is my biannual public service call for someone, *anyone* with a CPA in the United States, to help out the author community and produce practical resources to minimize our tax liability.

Yes, I know it's not sexy, and yes, I know, most authors don't care about taxes.

But I do. I finally hired a CPA this year to help me with my bookkeeping and taxes. We meet monthly, I can call him whenever I have a question, and he does my taxes at the end of the year. And it's expensive. Not every author can afford this kind of service.

Nothing beats a competent CPA who has experience in the author community, but there's a lot of basic information that authors need to know. Taxes isn't just about what you can deduct. There's a lot more to it.

In the previous volume, I recommended someone creating a business called "Your Self-Publishing Accountant." I suggested that this person could carve out a space in the community by offering free tax advice, affordable ebooks, and even paid courses.

Back in 2015, a writer with a CPA started this but stopped for unknown reasons. They published a book that they updated each year with tax law changes. This author also led small virtual workshops during tax season where attendees could ask questions. It was immensely helpful to me as a newbie who knew nothing about taxes or business.

I also believe such a platform would be helpful to new authors today.

Books

The Reader's Bill of Rights

Every reader has 11 inalienable rights. Respect these rights and you'll transform ordinary readers into superfans. Violate these rights and you'll lose readers and a lot of money. This book is a manifesto on how to treat your readers right and how to stand out in today's crowded market where most authors are taking their fans for granted.

Buy at www.authorlevelup.com/billofrights

250+ Writing Tips, Vol. 1

.   .   .

This book contains a breath-taking amount of writing, marketing, and publishing tips that will level up your author game. Inspired by Michael's podcast "Writing Tip of the Day," the tips are concise and practical so you can implement them right away.

Buy at www.authorlevelup.com/tips1

The Indie Author Atlas

This imaginative travel guide takes all of the important lessons you need to learn as an aspiring author and turns them into can't-miss vacation destinations across five continents. Journey to The Commonwealth of Craft to discover the secrets of the writing masters, hike through the mountainous land of Market-stan and learn how to market like a boss, and even stop by the sacred lands of Distribution to witness how you can maximize your books' earning potential. You won't find another writing book like this one.

Buy at www.authorlevelup.com/atlas

The Indie Author Bestiary

The hardest side of the writing life is the emotional one. This book takes the emotional "beasts" of the writing world, converts them into actual monsters, and teaches you how to slay them.

Michael will be your guide as you embark on an epic quest against writer's block, fear, self-doubt, and more.

Buy at www.authorlevelup.com/bestiary

The Author Income Problem

Do you stare at a mountain of sales reports every month and sweat about how you're going to calculate your sales? This book will outline how you can track your sales without pulling your hair out. While the solution requires some hard work, you'll glean insights into your sales data that will give you an unfair advantage in today's market where most authors don't even bother with it. The only question you should be asking is: how much money are you leaving on the table by NOT conquering your sales reports?

Buy at www.authorlevelup.com/theauthorincomeproblem

Author Level Up YouTube Channel - Highlights

Watch at youtube.com/authorlevelup.

Writing While on the Road: Watch over Michael's shoulder as he writes books while on vacation and still manages to get an astonishing amount of work done.

. . .

Michael's 2021 Strategy Livestream: Michael outlines his plans for 2021 in painstaking detail.

How to beat fear and self-doubt: An honest talk about how to face the demons of the writing life.

Interviews & Appearances

Mental Models for Authors and the Empowered Author with Michael La Ronn (The Creative Penn): In Michael's second appearance on The Creative Penn, Michael and Joanna discuss a range of interesting topics including mental models, artificial intelligence, and how to be a writing machine.

Control Your Writing Destiny with Michael La Ronn (Growing Intentions Blog): An interview about what it means to be a writer. (Link no longer active).

Guest Interview with Michael La Ronn (Dark Neon Blog): An intimidate discussion about writing craft.

The Power of Storytelling with Michael La Ronn (Hidden Falls Media Podcast): An in-depth discussion about marketing, something Michael has never talked about on a podcast interview before.

.   .   .

An Introduction to Scrivener with Michael La Ronn (REWRITE London): Join Michael as he gives an hour-long introduction to Scrivener to a virtual workshop.

How to Use Scrivener to Write Your Novel with Michael La Ronn (REWRITE London): Join Michael as he goes deeper into Scrivener and how to use it at every step of the writing process.

READ THE NEXT VOLUME

Michael's writer journey continues in the next volume of this series!

Grab your copy at www.authorlevelup.com/confidential.

MEET M.L. RONN

Science fiction and fantasy on the wild side!

M.L. Ronn (Michael La Ronn) is the author of many science fiction and fantasy novels including *The Good Necromancer, Android X,* and *The Last Dragon Lord* series.

In 2012, a life-threatening illness made him realize that storytelling was his #1 passion. He's devoted his life to writing ever since, making up whatever story makes him fall out of his chair laughing the hardest. Every day.

Learn more about Michael
www.authorlevelup.com (for writers)
www.michaellaronn.com (fiction)

MORE BOOKS BY M.L. RONN

Books for Writers:

www.authorlevelup.com/books

Fiction:
www.michaellaronn.com/books